Treasure Island Revisited

*The Newfoundland story that inspired
Robert Louis Stevenson's Treasure Island*

Treasure Island Revisited

Jack Fitzgerald

St. John's, Newfoundland and Labrador
2005

©2005, Jack Fitzgerald

We acknowledge the support of The Canada Council for the Arts for our publishing program.

We acknowledge the financial support of the Government of Canada through the Book Publishing Industry Development Program (BPIDP) for our publishing program.

Cover Design: Maurice Fitzgerald
∞ Printed on acid-free paper

Published by
CREATIVE PUBLISHERS
an imprint of CREATIVE BOOK PUBLISHING
a division of Creative Printers and Publishers Limited
a Transcontinental associated company
P.O. Box 8660, St. John's, Newfoundland A1B 3T7

First Edition
Typeset in 12 point Goudy Old Style

Printed in Canada by:
TRANSCONTINENTAL PRINT

National Library of Canada Cataloguing in Publication

Fitzgerald, Jack, 1945-
        Treasure Island revisited / Jack Fitzgerald.

ISBN 1-894294-89-0

        1. Keating, John, Captain. 2. Treasure-trove--Costa Rica--Cocos Island. 3. Pirates--Peru--Lima. I. Title.

F2161.F56 2005   910.4'5   C2005-903514-5

Dedication

Dedicated to Jillian, a treasure more glowing than
"The Lost Treasure of Lima."

Poppy Jack

Appreciation

Researching and writing *Treasure Island Revisited* was both a challenge and a real labour of love. For those who offered help and inspiration along the way, I extend my sincere appreciation.

I was fortunate in having the assistance of my friend Bob Rumsey, a retired English teacher, in the several revisions this book went through before it was ready for the publisher. This process took long hours of checking, rechecking and rewriting, plus numerous consultations regarding the flow and continuity of the story. Bob's help was invaluable.

I thank Dr. Ina Knobloch of Frankfurt, Germany for providing the inspiration to take on the task of delving into the Newfoundland connection to the wonderful story of the Lost Treasure of Lima and Cocos Island, the real *Treasure Island*.

The staff at the Maritime History Archives, Memorial University, were kind enough to give me a crash course in searching their Maritime History Records, and were most cooperative and helpful at all times. It was information I found at the MHA that enabled me to clear up many of the mysteries related to the Lima Treasure story, and to bring forward a great deal of new information.

I am also thankful to the staff members at the Provincial Archives of Newfoundland and Labrador, the Newfoundland Collection room at the Hunter Library in St. John's, NL, the Newfoundland Studies Unit at the Queen Elizabeth II Library at MUN, St. John's, NL, and the staff at the City of St. John's Archives.

I thank my friend Dick Hartery for his encouragement and suggestions, my son Maurice for cover design and authors photographs and other suggestions which were helpful. Also, thanks to Don Morgan for his final editing work on *Treasure Island Revisited*.

Special thanks to Donna Francis, Angela Pitcher, and the staff at Creative Publishers for their enthusiasm, support and patience in preparing and getting this book to the general public.

Table of Contents

Introduction..viii

Foreword ix

Chapter 1: The Lost Treasure of Lima.....................................1

Chapter 2: Keating gets the Treasure Map.............................14

Chapter 3: Keating Finds Lost Treasure of Lima................30

Chapter 4: Enter Captain Nick Fitzgerald.............................44

Chapter 5: Clues to the Treasure 62

Chapter 6: Stevenson's Ben Gun 86

Chapter 7: Shysters and Adventurers...................................101

Chapter 8: The True Pirate and Treasure.............................125

Chapter 9: Stevenson's *Treasure Island* 140

Author's Notes:..147

Bibliography 157

Introduction

Few subjects excite our imaginations as intensely as the lore of hidden treasure. For the adventurous, the knowledge of a possible location is addictive. The unreliability of information, often associated with the passage of time, seldom discourages the true believer. The quest, more often than not for gold, is prone to haunt, rather than to satisfy, the dedicated seeker.

A routine visit to the government archives in St. John's, Newfoundland led to the recording of a tale of an association between our province and an idyllic island three hundred miles off the coast of Costa Rica. The account of Newfoundland's involvement with Cocos Island was included in Jack Fitzgerald's book *Beyond Belief,* published in 2001. It was destined to remain simply another revelation of the unusual in our history until Dr. Ina Knobloch, a German writer and television producer, read it. She was researching Cocos Island for a documentary she was making on its reputation as a site of multiple treasure-troves. In *Beyond Belief,* she learned of John Keating, a Newfoundlander, and his colleague, Captain Thompson, both of whom were unquestionably linked to the alleged fortunes of Cocos Island. Dr. Knobloch, having contacted Jack, decided to travel to St. John's in July of 2004. While there, she became immersed in the additional material which resulted from Jack's ongoing investigation. Undoubtedly, she was impressed by the author's effort to piece together the puzzle of two islands, seemingly unrelated, but for a brief period of time, very much connected.

Before returning home, Dr. Knobloch asked Jack to accompany her and her film crew to the mysterious Pacific island. Unfortunately, he was unable to accept her offer.

Treasure Island Revisited is the result of persistent meticulous probing, an admirable endeavour to expose the truth of the legends of an island previously unknown to the majority of us. This book will grip the concentration of treasure hunters and utterly entertain less serious readers.

Robert 'Bob' Rumsey
Retired school teacher, St. John's, NL

Foreword

We find the name of Captain John Keating in more than twenty books on pirates and great treasures, yet he is all but forgotten in Newfoundland and Labrador — the country of his birth. In my book *Beyond Belief,* I included a short story entitled *Captain John Keating's Secret.* This story tells how Captain Keating was given a map by an old pirate named Thompson, who died in St. John's, and how Keating went on to Cocos Island to successfully find a treasure trove.

Although the name John Keating is known world wide among those interested in the secrets of Cocos Island, very little is known of the man himself. In *The Great Treasure Hunts*, 1968, Rupert Furneaux wrote:

> Almost everyone who has heard of Cocos Island knows the name of John Keating, *the mystery man of Newfoundland*, to whom Thompson imparted the secret of the treasure hidden there in a cave.

Treasure Island Revisited removes the veil of secrecy that has surrounded John Keating's name for almost two centuries, and reveals his story for the first time.

During April 2004, I was at home putting the finishing touches on my recently published book, *Untold Stories of Newfoundland*, when my publisher phoned, telling me to expect a call from a German television producer. The producer was interested in a story I had included in my book *Beyond Belief.* Naturally, I was puzzled.

Five minutes later the phone rang, and it was Dr. Ina Knobloch, the German television producer who had called my publisher earlier. I was a little surprised when I learned it was my story of Keating that interested her, and I was even more surprised when she asked if she could bring a television crew to St. John's to interview me. I agreed, and the filming was scheduled for the last week of July, 2004.

Over the following few weeks my interest in Keating increased, and I learned that what had been known in Newfoundland history as the Cocos Island Treasure story, was better known around the world as the story of the Lost Treasure of Lima. Another intriguing aspect of the Lima Treasure was that it was being described as one of the largest unfound treasures in the world. Writers were estimating its current value at three hundred million dollars. Even more fascinating was the popular belief that the story of the Lost Treasure of Lima had inspired Robert Louis Stevenson to write his classic novel, *Treasure Island*.

I turned my full attention to preparing for the interview, and set out to learn as much as I could about Keating. By July I had gathered quite a collection of material on Keating, the Cocos Island, and the Lost Treasure of Lima. Having researched the Keating/Cocos Island story, I was able to uncover previously unknown material to confirm the rumors of Keating's knowledge of the Cocos Island, and his efforts to recover its treasures. By the time I met Dr. Knobloch, I felt convinced that the story of Captain John Keating was one of Newfoundland history's greatest adventure stories. It was then that I decided to write a book on the Lost Treasure of Lima and its strong connection to Newfoundland.

The end result was the amassing of a great deal of new information, and the solution to many of the questions that had plagued writers over the past hundred years, who had kept the story of Keating and the Lost Treasure of Lima alive. Two areas of research I pursued which had not been touched by others were the Lloyd's of London Shipping Records and Newfoundland archival material. The Lloyd's records, which include indexes, shipping movements and registries, are stored at the Maritime History Archives, Memorial University, St. John's, Newfoundland. The Newfoundland archival material for this book was found at the Provincial Archives of Newfoundland and Labrador, the Newfoundland Collection at the Hunter Library; the Centre for Newfoundland and

Labrador Studies at the Queen Elizabeth II Library, and the City of St. John's Archives. These sources revealed much new information about Newfoundland's involvement in the Lima Treasure story.

Meanwhile, Dr. Knobloch's research in Europe and South America was stirring up interest throughout the world. The various archives in St. John's began receiving inquiries about Captain John Keating, from writers as far away as Costa Rica.

The Newfoundland portion of the documentary was filmed at Government House, the Colonial Building, and the Maritime History Archives. The German Television crew also filmed at the little cemetery near the entrance of Bay Bulls Harbour, and at Belvedere Cemetery in St. John's. Filming was also done at the Newfoundland Museum, the St. John's Waterfront, and on the *Scademia*, as it sailed from St. John's to Freshwater Bay on a hot, humid evening in July 2004.

Dr. Knobloch was pleased with the information obtained in Newfoundland, and in appreciation extended an invitation to me to join their December 2004 expedition to Cocos Island to complete their documentary. The trip on the *Okeanos Aggressor* — used in the recent NBC Dateline feature *Thrill Seekers* — was also expected to be the last treasure hunting expedition to Stevenson's Treasure Island. The island is now a World Heritage Site, and treasure hunting is no longer permitted. However, the Costa Rican government issued a permit to the German group to simulate a dig for the purpose of filming the documentary.

Just a week before I was to leave St. John's to meet the German televison crew at San Jose, Costa Rica, a health problem prevented me from traveling.

Two documentaries have been made from the film gathered by Dr. Knobloch for release in July 2005, with initial plans to translate them into German and French for distribution in Europe. There is a future possibility of the program being translated into English for distribution in Canada.

Chapter 1

The Lost Treasure of Lima

The inspiration for Robert Louis Stevenson's Treasure Island is believed to be the story of the Lost Treasure of Lima, hidden on Cocos Island.

"From John Keating has descended the fundamental Cocos legend which is accepted by all modern Treasure Hunters."

– Rupert Furneaux, The Great Treasure Hunts, 1968

The *Edgecombe* had arrived in Chatham Bay, Cocos Island on June 18, 1841. The carefully guarded secret of the leaders of this expedition was soon to unravel. Cocos Island, the destination which was part of this secret, was an uninhabited island 300 miles off the coast of Costa Rica. They had come to recover the Lost Treasure of Lima. How the treasure was stolen from Lima and buried on Cocos Island, and its connection with Newfoundland, is a story that had its beginning in the Spanish American Revolution.

In 1821 South Americans were in revolt against Spanish rule. Chili had succeeded in driving the Spanish out of Chilean territory and had assumed a leading role in driving the Spanish Royalists out of neighboring Peru. The Chilean Government placed General Jose de San Martin in command of its army, and Lord Thomas Cochrane, the tenth Earl of Dundonald and former British Naval Commander, in charge of its Navy. The Chilean Army was comprised of 1800 Chileans and 2400 Argentine volunteers. Although the navy had less than a dozen ships, Cochrane had the reputation of being a supreme naval strategist. Cochrane, however, had not been pleased when the Government placed San Martin in charge of the military action against the Spanish.

In 1820 San Martin had signed an armistice with General Jose de La Serna, Commander of the Spanish Forces in Peru. By the end of that year the armistice had failed, and in January 1821, San Martin and Cochrane were concentrating on ousting the Spanish from Lima. Cochrane took his ships to the port of Callao, the port city of Lima, where he quickly captured the *Esmeralda*, a Spanish man-o'-war, and the only

Spanish Naval vessel in port. Following this action, he enforced a naval blockade of Callao. La Serna took his Royalist troops into the interior, leaving only a small garrison at Rey Felipe Castle, the ancient fort at Callao. La Serna planned on continuing his struggle against the patriots from the interior. He left Captain Manuel Abreau in command at Callao.

Inside the city of Lima the population was in a state of panic. The evacuation of the Royalist Army had left the residents in terror, particularly the middle and upper classes. They were convinced that the city was surrounded by wild Indians, violent former slaves, criminals, and terrorists.[1]

The population was well aware of the immense wealth stored in the city, which was in addition to the personal wealth of its citizens. Lima was the seat of Spanish power in the western world and the capital of wealth and culture. There was probably more gold and silver within the walls of Lima than had ever been gathered together in any colonial city in the history of the world. During the last decades of the colonial period in South America, Peru accounted for almost sixty percent of the total value of gold mined in Spanish America.[2]

In August 1821, Captain Abreau organized an impromptu effort to save as much of the accumulated wealth in the city of Lima as possible. The plan was to cart the treasure to the Rey Felipe Castle, which was protected by a small garrison of Royalists. In a swift operation, they removed gold, silver, and gems from the Roman Catholic Cathedral, the wealth held by civic authorities, and as much of the individual wealth of the dons and grandees as the troops could handle.

The scene on the road to Callao that day was described by the author A. Hyatt Verril in his book *Lost Treasure*. He wrote:

> Great was the hurrying and scurrying of the wealthy merchants, the rich planters and mine owners, the gold-laced officials, the gilded idlers and the ton-

1. *The Independence of Spanish America*, James Rodriguez, 1998
2. *Doubloons*, Charles H. Driscoll, 1931

sured friars, as they gathered their hoards of treasure, and on pack-mules, donkeys, horses, and the backs of Indians; in carts, barrows and coaches, they carried it over the rutty, dusty road to Callao and saw it safely stored within the massive walls of the Felipe Citadel.

Photo Courtesy the Frank "Spotty" Baird collection

Millions of dollars in gold, silver, and gems were removed from this Cathedral in August, 1821, and stored aboard the *Mary Dear* under the command of Captain William Thompson.

While the citizens of Lima and the Royalist garrison at Callao prepared for the worst, friction was growing between San Martin and Cochrane over San Martin's military strategy. San Martin wanted victory without military confrontation, and argued that they were in the country to free Peru — not to occupy it. He was convinced that the Peruvians would rise up and support him when he entered Lima. Cochrane, on the other hand, felt their strategy should be to aggressively pursue the Spanish forces. He was convinced that San Martin's thinking was being negatively affected by his daily use of opium to dull the pain of his tuberculosis.

Another sore point between the two commanding officers was money. Cochrane was aware that San Martin had looted silver from the Cerro de Pasco mines in Peru on his march to

Lima, but refused to share this wealth. Lord Cochrane claimed he was in need of money to pay his troops and wondered how long he could control them under such circumstances.[3]

Throughout this crisis, Peru was dependent on foreign shipping for its supplies and to ship products to outside markets. Abandoned by the Royalists army, civic officials in Lima invited San Martin to enter the city as its Protector to provide law and order. San Martin was not interested in plundering the treasures of Lima. He offered amnesty to Royalists wishing to leave, and permitted them to take their wealth with them. Cochrane, however, demanded one-third of the treasure being taken out of the port of Callao in return for the safe passage of any ship.[4] In addition to this, he seized San Martin's private yacht, and removed a treasure of ingots of solid gold and pieces of eight. (A 'piece of eight' was a coin called the Spanish Real. The coin was scored so that it could be broken into eight pieces, each valued at 12 ½ cents.)[5]

There was an overwhelming response to the amnesty offer. Those with wealth approached the ships' Captains in Callao with generous offers of money to help them get out of Peru with their wealth. Most wanted to be taken to Spain. Captain Abrau, now in charge of Callao, met with Captain Thompson of the *Mary Dear* with a request for help in saving the treasure which was stored in the Cathedral of Lima. The *Mary Dear* was flying a British flag, which gave it an advantage in Pacific waters. Spain was at war with Britain, and most of the Spanish Navy had been driven out of the Pacific. The British flag would have been respected by South American naval vessels. An agreement worked out between Captain Thompson and Royalist Captain Abrau assured Thompson a generous fee for his assistance. A guard, made up of four Spanish soldiers and two priests from the Cathedral of Lima, was sent on board to help protect and assure safe delivery of

3. *Doubloons*, Charles H. Driscoll, 1931
4. *Doubloons*, Charles H. Driscoll, 1931
5. Lloyd's of London Shipping Movements 1821, Maritime History Archives, Memorial University, St. John's, NL; and McAlpine's *Newfoundland Directory*, 1871.

the treasure. The final destination of the *Mary Dear* was to be given to Thompson by the officer in charge of the guard only after the vessel was at sea.

Some of the ships that left Callao during the amnesty made it to Spain, while others fell prey to pirates on the Pacific Coast and in the Caribbean. The danger to the *Mary Dear,* however, did not come from outside the vessel. The presence of so much gold, silver, and gems turned the thoughts of its crew to piracy. Those thoughts simmered for hours, then turned to a united action. The men respected and feared Captain Marion Thompson, but they were determined not to let him stand in their way. Each, with one hand on his pistol and the other on his cutlass, approached the Captain to give him the ultimatum, "Join us or die with the guards."

Courtesy Maritime History Archives, MUN
Nfld. Fish Boxes: A Chronicle of the Fishery
Dr. Harry Roberts with Michael Knowlan, 1982.

The *Mary Dear* may have been similar in design to the brig shown in this picture. This brig was in use during the period from 1850 to 1855.

Thompson was also being moved by greed, and must have welcomed the decision his crew had taken. He had already decided to steal the treasure, and was about to enlist the crew's support. With captain and crew united in a purpose, they determined that the deed of piracy would not be implemented until they had left port. Thompson felt they would have a better chance to escape by following this course of action. At night the *Mary Dear* slipped anchor, and escaped unnoticed from the Royalist-controlled harbour. In waters off the coast of Peru, and out of sight of Cochrane's forces, Thompson led his men in cutting the throats of the guards and priests and tossing their bodies into the ocean.

The total value of treasure in Callao at the time was estimated to be seventy million dollars. The amount of treasure taken from the Cathedral of Lima and stored on the *Mary Dear* was about twelve million dollars. A large part of the Lima Treasure remained hidden inside the fort. It had been secretly buried there by Spanish soldiers who intended to keep it for themselves. These soldiers did not live to recover their loot, as they died in battles in the interior.

On September 19, 1821, a month after the piracy of the Lima Treasure, San Martin took possession of Callao, and raised the Patriot Flag over the fort. According to author Charles H. Driscoll, San Martin found and looted the remaining portion of the Lima Treasure hidden inside the fort.

While there is disagreement over the value of the treasure stolen by Thompson in 1821, most writers' listings mention the following items as being included:

> 753 bars of gold, (four by three inches wide), an undisclosed number of silver bars, gold and silver coins, gold chalices, candlesticks and statues, one or two life-size gold statues of the Madonna and child, gem encrusted church ornaments, emeralds and sapphire jewelry, gem encrusted clergy vestments and hand carved gold plates stolen from the Incas.

Some years later a letter was made public by the Cocos Island Treasure Company, which they claimed had been written by Captain Thompson. The letter described what had happened after the *Mary Dear* pirated the Lima Treasure. Although the origin of the letter may be questionable, some of its content is consistent with most of the authentic records of the event. In this letter Thompson describes what happened after the theft of the treasure. He stated:

> The next morning at daylight, we saw that we were chased by an armed vessel. Our ship was a fast sailing vessel, and everything alow and aloft was in first class order. Although it was blowing pretty hard, we hoisted every stitch of canvas and gained on the pursuing vessel. The next morning at daybreak we were clear of her. We shortened sail and now had another problem to solve. What should we do with the treasure? Many plans were proposed and as quickly rejected. At last, we agreed to bury the stuff on Cocos Island.
>
> Coming to the island, the treasure was conveyed in ten boat loads to the beach. Then we looked for a place to bury it. Reaching back from the shore, where we made our landing, was a piece of level ground about two acres. This ground laid on the foot of a mountain. Down its side ran a stream. We followed the stream very near to its head, on the level ground at the foot of the mountain. Here we selected the spot, and after distributing a share to each man, buried the treasure. Some was in boxes and some in hides and it was supposed to be worth many millions.

Captain Thompson told his crew that they were now pirates and there was no turning back. He said there was enough gold to look after all of them in their old age, and as well to ensure the future of their children. He reminded them that they could not touch the main treasure for some years until after authorities had given up their pursuit. To throw his searchers off his trail after leaving Cocos Island, he brought the *Mary Dear* close to the coast of Mexico. There he set the ship ablaze and led his band of pirates in abandoning the ship.[6]

6. *Doubloons,* Charles H. Driscoll, 1931; and *The World Atlas of Treasure,* Derek Wilson, 1981

In his book, *True Tales of Pirates and Their Gold*, Edward R. Snow claimed that treasure had not been stolen from Lima. However, Rupert Furneaux, in his book *The Great Treasure Hunts,* quoted excerpts from Lord Thomas Cochrane's diary to prove that a great treasure had been stolen from Lima by the *Mary Dear* and its crew. He wrote:

> On the approach of San Martin, the Viceroy and the ecclesiastical dignitaries, fearful for the riches of their churches, decided to transport their wealth to Callao to await shipment away from the threatened area. That this was done is vouched for by Admiral Cochrane who noted in his diary on 19 August 1821; 'The Spaniards today relieved and reinforced the fortress of Callao, and coolly walked off unmolested with plate and money to the amount of many millions of pounds — in fact, the whole wealth of Lima which was deposited in the fort for safe keeping.'

Referring to the aftermath of the Lima Treasure theft, Furneaux wrote:

> What happened next is an historical fact, for the Spaniards broadcast throughout their dominions a 'hue and cry' notice for the apprehension of the *Mary Dear* and her piratical crew.

Lloyd's of London Records of Shipping Movements for the period from 1821 to 1824 indicates a concerted effort to track down pirates following the theft of the Treasure of Lima.

Additional confirmation of the theft of the Lima Treasure comes from Herve de Montmorency, in his book *On The Track of Treasure*. The author was a close friend of British Admiral Palliser, and the two joined together in a 1902 expedition to find the treasure. Henry L. Palliser visited Cocos

Island in 1896, while still active with the Royal Navy. He had used his ship and men to search for the treasure, and during that effort had used dynamite to move rocks. This episode resulted in a reprimand from the British Government, and caused the Royal Navy to ban the use of all Naval ships in future Cocos Island expeditions. Palliser's interest in the Lima Treasure was sparked by the things he had learned from two associates, the President of the Peruvian Republic, and the Governor of the Bank of Lima. Palliser had met the two leaders while serving as an admiral in charge of British Naval activities in South America.

The President had told the British admiral of immense treasures stolen from Peru and buried on Cocos Island. The Governor of the Lima Bank also related stories of pirate treasures on Cocos Island, but was more specific. He mentioned a twelve million dollar treasure stolen by the captain of the *Mary Dear*. According to Palliser, Lima historical records relate the facts of the capture, trial, and sentencing of Thompson's companions.

Photo, Carter-Fitzgerald Black & White Photography

Jack Fitzgerald researching Spanish American Revolution at the Queen Elizabeth II Library, Memorial University, St. John's, Newfoundland.

Thompson and his band of pirates made it to Mexico. However, news of the piracy of the Lima Treasure, and the murder of the guards and priests had already reached that country. They were captured as they attempted to go ashore. Captain Thompson, a smooth talker with access to untold wealth, succeeded in bribing his captors to allow him and his crew to escape.[7]

From Mexico, Thompson and his band of murderers and thieves made it to Panama where they pirated a small vessel. They now began adding to their hidden wealth on Cocos Island. The buccaneers terrorized the coast of California, Mexico, and sometimes expanded their activities to the Caribbean.[8] Over the next year the following ships along the Western Pacific were taken by pirates, possibly Thompson: *The Rose In Bloom, The Congress, The Luzetan, The Baron de Court, The Azima,* and several passenger ships. Hundreds of thousands of dollars in cash, gold and silver were taken.[9]

When Thompson's ship became inadequate for substantial pirate activities, he attempted to take a large vessel. The plan failed when a British Naval ship intercepted and captured Thompson and his crew. The prisoners were taken to Cuba where all except Thompson and his mate, a man named Chapelle, were put to death. Thompson's charm and persuasion, which had served him so well in the past, once again succeeded in helping him and Chapelle escape the gallows. He convinced his captors that he and Chapelle could take them to the Lima Treasure buried on Cocos Island. The British agreed to the offer and took the two pirates to Cocos Island to lead them to the hiding place of the Lima Treasure.

There is a possibility that it was Lord Cochrane who brought the two pirates to Cocos Island on that occasion. While Lord Cochrane's diary indicates he met with pirates on

---

7. *World Atlas of Treasure*, Derek Wilson, 1981
8. *Newfoundland Quarterly,* 1908 article by Inspector General of Newfoundland Constabulary, Charles H. Hutchings
9. Lloyd's of London Shipping Movements 1821, 1822, and 1823, Maritime History Archives, Memorial University of Newfoundland.

Cocos Island during December of 1822, he does not identify the names of the pirates.[10]

Captain Marion Thompson knew that once the treasure was located, he and Chapelle would be hung or shot like the others. The cunning Thompson led the men deep into the jungle and pointed out a cave in a small rock face. Then, as the excited sailors hurried forward, he and Chapelle slipped into the thick brushwood and vanished. They were out of sight before their escape was noticed. The two fugitives were hunted like animals for three days, but Thompson had the advantage of knowing the Island. The two found refuge in a cave behind a waterfall, and lay there until the British captain gave up the chase and sailed away.[11]

Thompson and Chapelle survived for several months on fish, roots, coconuts and palm hearts. The two were finally rescued by the crew of a whaler that had stopped at Chatham Bay to load fresh water, and they were taken to Puntarenas.

Thompson made his way to Hawaii, and later Samoa, where he settled down and changed his name to McComber. Records are not clear on whether or not Chapelle followed him. During subsequent years, several claims emerged from the Samoa-Hawaii area claiming that either Chapelle or Thompson had spoken about the treasure on Cocos Island, and in a few cases maps to the hiding place of the treasure, which were alleged to be authentic, were produced. However, no credible evidence regarding Thompson's whereabouts surfaced until early in 1840, at Metanzas, Cuba.

W & H Thomas, shipping merchants at St. John's, Newfoundland, sent the *Mercury*, under Captain John Humphries, with a cargo for Cuba. On board the vessel was Captain John Keating, who was also a respected ship carpenter in St. John's. He had gone on the voyage to Cuba, at the request of the owners of the *Mercury*, to monitor a problem

10. Dr. Ina Knobloch, Frankfurt, Germany, 2004
11. *The Romance of Treasure,* T.C. Bridges, 1931

the vessel was experiencing at sea, and to correct it if necessary.

By chance, Keating met a stranger at a public inn while in Metanzas and the two engaged in conversation. The stranger identified himself as Captain Thompson and in the conversation that followed, revealed that he knew St. John's well because he had been there many times in his early sea-going years.

A crewman on the *Mercury* had died on its voyage to Cuba, and Captain Humphries was looking for someone to replace him. When Thompson learned of this, he expressed an interest in going to Newfoundland and asked Keating if he would speak to Captain Humphries on his behalf. The two left the inn and made their way through the dark, dusty streets of Metanzas to the *Mercury*. The ship's captain was happy to have an experienced seaman offer himself for work and Thompson was welcomed aboard.

Courtesy Maritime History Archives, MUN
Nfld. Fish Boxes: A Chronicle of the Fishery
Dr. Harry Roberts with Michael Knowlan, 1982.

This ship, tossing about in a North Atlantic storm, is similar in design to the *Mercury*.

Chapter 2

Keating Gets the Treasure Map

"Here's to ourselves
and hold your luff
plenty of prizes and
plenty of duff."

Long John Silver, Treasure Island

During the trip to Newfoundland Thompson developed a close and trusting friendship with John Keating and in confidence told him the story of how he had pirated and buried the treasure of Lima on an Island in the South Pacific. He suggested to Keating that if Keating could find backers for an expedition to the island, he could make every man involved very rich. Keating was a little skeptical of the story at first and asked him why he had kept the secret to himself for such a long period. The pirate explained that he was in fear of what might happen to him if the authorities got wind of the story and identified him. Thompson said that he had to be very cautious because he was a wanted man in every port.

While coming to St. John's on the *Mercury,* Thompson had asked Keating about the availability of accommodation for him while in St. John's. Keating answered that his wife operated a lodging house on Duckworth Street, near the waterfront and the Customs House, and Thompson would be a welcome guest. The pirate gladly accepted Keating's invitation. By the time the voyage ended, the two had become trusted friends and Keating not only believed the story, but was anxious to participate in an expedition to recover the treasure.[1] He knew two merchants in St. John's who could be trusted and who might have the kind of money needed to finance a treasure-hunting expedition.

The *Mercury* arrived in St. John's Harbour on May 9, 1840. Keating wasted little time in going ashore and arranging a meeting with merchants Richard Perchard and James Boag. These two men were partners in the merchant shipping firm

1. *The Romance of Treasure,* T.C. Bridges, 1931

known as Messrs. Perchard and Boag, which had a fleet of nearly two dozen ships. The meeting was arranged at the home of James Boag with Thompson and Keating present. There, Thompson told his story of piracy and of a buried treasure just waiting to be recovered.

Winter scene at St. John's harbour—early nineteenth century.

Captain Thompson had also shared with Keating the secret hiding place of a second treasure, which was possibly even larger than the Lost Treasure of Lima. He told Keating how he had served under the notorious pirate Captain Benito "Bloody Sword" Bonito and was with him when he buried a fortune in stolen treasure, much of it taken from Lima. Thompson claimed that he was one of only two survivors of Bonito's pirate crew.[2] It is not clear if the story of the Bonito Treasure was ever told to the merchants.

Thompson suggested to the merchants that if they would furnish him with a vessel, he could ballast it with money and treasures from Cocos Island. If he couldn't, they could shoot him. The former pirate captain added, "This would be easy with only one man against the crew."

When Perchard asked him how far the treasure was from the water, he answered, "Come to the island and see for your-

2. *The Book of Buried Treasure*, Ralph D. Paine, 1922. *The Romance of Buried Treasure*, T.C. Bridges, 1931

self how far it is from the water, but I'll not tell you before." Perchard and Boag promised to consider the venture and suggested they meet again.

Thompson may have had another reason for coming to St. John's, and rather than the visit having resulted from an accidental encounter with Keating at Metanzas, it may have been a planned and calculated move by the old pirate. Lord Thomas Cochrane, the 10th Earl of Dundonald, had taken one third of the treasure in Lima in 1821, just before Thompson pirated his portion of the treasure. A month or so later, the Earl stole the entire treasure of Peru, which had been stored at Ancon. His diary states that during December 22, 1822, he met with a pirate on Cocos Island, possibly Captain Marion Thompson. These are circumstances that add fuel to the theory that Thompson and Cochrane may have come to some sort of agreement regarding the loot.

Given the background of both men, it is quite possible that they knew each other long before the piracy of the Lima Treasure. They were both from Scotland, both sailed at the same period in the West Indies and both were on the Pacific Coast of South America at the same time. While enforcing a blockade of the port of Callao, Cochrane allowed Thompson to leave port with the *Mary Dear* laden down with treasure.

In 1832, Lord Cochrane became Commander-in-Chief of the Royal Navy North American Station. In this position he would have spent a great deal of time in St. John's and would have frequented Government House, constructed in 1828, by another Lord Cochrane, who was Governor of Newfoundland and possibly a nephew of Lord Cochrane, the 10th Earl of Dundonald.

Dr. Ina Knobloch, producer of a German Television documentary on the treasures of Cocos Island, raised some interesting questions regarding the relationship between the pirate Thompson and the Earl of Dundonald. For example, "Did the Earl and Thompson know each other? Was the Earl pos-

sibly involved in concealing the Lima Treasure? Was any of it
hidden in St. John's, perhaps on the grounds at Government
House? Did Thompson actually come to St. John's to seek out
Lord Cochrane, or to find any treasure that Cochrane may
have hidden?

In relationship to these aspects of the Lost Treasure of
Lima story, the German television crew arrived at
Government House an hour early on the day of scheduled
filming and shot footage of the outside areas as possible hid-
ing places for any of the treasure that had been brought to
Newfoundland by the Earl of Dundonald.

At the second meeting, between the merchants and treasure
seekers, Captain James Boag told Keating and Thompson that
he had checked the story and had found Thompson's statements to be quite correct; however, the venture would have to
wait awhile because his firm could not spare the money at that
time. Keating was not happy with the lack of enthusiasm
shown by the merchants. When an old and trusted friend of
his, Captain William Boag — not connected with the Perchard
& Boag firm — arrived in port on the ship *George Henry
Harrison* a few days later on May 16th. Keating seized the
opportunity to try and involve his friend.

William Boag was a veteran sea captain. He had sailed the
seven seas for firms in Newfoundland and England.[3]
Although he was not connected to the Perchard-Boag firm, he
was likely related to Captain James Boag. Keating felt confident that he could persuade Captain William Boag to participate and help plan the treasure hunting expedition. He
brought Thompson on board the ship to meet Boag and the
three held a long and private meeting.

Boag displayed an enthusiasm which the merchants
Perchard and Boag had lacked and he was confident he could
find backers for the expedition in Liverpool, England, where
he had many business contacts. Nevertheless, he had several

3. In nineteenth century St. John's, the name Boag was sometimes spelled as "Boig".

ports to visit before returning there and he would not arrive
in England until sometime in October 1840.

Captain Keating remained busy while awaiting the outcome of Boag's efforts in Liverpool. He took a job as Captain
of the *Alexander* and delivered cargoes between St. John's and
Halifax from August to October 1840.

Water Street during the nineteenth century. The firm of Perchard and Boag operated
their shipping business from a building on this street.

During his stay in St. John's, Thompson had charmed his way
into the city's high society. He was never short of money and
was popular with the ladies of the city, especially the daughter
of the Governor. In *The Book of Buried Treasure*, Ralph D.
Paine described Thompson as, "A man of middle age, hand-
some in appearance and having about him something of an
air of mystery which had an attraction of its own."

By November Boag had arrived in Liverpool where he
approached the principals of the firm, Smith & Irwin. This
British firm was large and wealthy and owned dozens of ships
that traveled all over the world. The two businessmen showed

an intense interest in Boag's story of hidden treasure and the Lima loot, but they wanted more evidence to support the claim. They asked Boag to arrange a face-to-face meeting with the pirate, Captain Marion Thompson, to explore the opportunity further.

Captain Boag sent for Keating and Thompson to join him at Liverpool. Within a month they were in Liverpool, where Boag had scheduled a meeting with Smith & Irwin. The two merchants listened attentively as Thompson told his story. They frequently interrupted him to ask specific questions and took notes on the answers provided. When the meeting was over the merchants promised to advise Thompson of their decision after they had a chance to verify his story. Thompson had included in his story the names of ships he had pirated and described the cargo taken. The two used this time to cross-check the information obtained from Thompson with the records of Lloyd's of London. The merchants were satisfied that Thompson had been truthful and decided to back the treasure hunting expedition to Cocos Island. The decision was welcomed by Keating, Boag and Thompson and they joined in a toast to the success of the venture. One could imagine hearing in that room the words of Long John Silver, after planning a mutiny on the *Hispaniola:*

Here's to ourselves and hold your luff,
Plenty of prizes and plenty of duff.

Smith & Irwin selected a cargo ship named the *Edgecombe* for the South Pacific expedition. They knew the project would require a large investment. The *Edgecombe* would be out of the cargo service for a year or more, plus there was the cost of supporting the crew throughout the adventure. A requirement in the agreement to finance the expedition was that Smith & Irwin send a representative of their choice along to protect their interests. The man they would choose for the task would be scheduled to join the *Edgecombe* several months later at Rio de Janeiro. Thompson, Keating, and Boag returned from Liverpool to St. John's during December, 1840, with high expectations, and to prepare for the expedition.[4]

On his return to St. John's, Thompson renewed his friendship with the Governor's daughter, and his wit and intelligence helped him make more friends. He entertained the ladies with stories of adventure on the high seas, with a sprinkling of intriguing pirate stories — no doubt based on his own life.

Nineteenth century brig similar to the *Edgecombe*, used in the adventure to find the Lost Treasure of Lima.

While the *Edgecombe* was being prepared for the expedition, Thompson caught a chill and, despite being tended by a St. John's doctor, he passed away at Keating's home.[5] Several versions of his death have emerged over the years.

Newfoundland historian P. K. Devine tells a romantic story of how the pirate Thompson met his end. According to Devine, Thompson was invited to a ball at Government House by the daughter of Governor LeMarchant (sic). During the evening, she told him that local authorities had received a warning to watch out for a man fitting Thompson's descrip-

4. *Newfoundland Quarterly* 8 (3): 9-10, The Cocos Island Treasure 1908, article by
   Charles H. Hutchings; *The Book of Buried Treasure*, Ralph D. Paine, 1922
5. *The Romance of Treasure*, T.C. Bridges, 1931

tion, who was wanted in connection with piracy. Of course, Thompson remained calm and dismissed the news as being of no consequence to him.[6]

When he returned to his lodging that night, Thompson called Keating to his room. Highly agitated, the pirate told Keating that the authorities were closing in on him and he had to leave St. John's immediately. He then gave his map of the treasure on Cocos Island to Keating, and said he would contact him again in the spring to finalize plans for the expedition. If Thompson didn't make it, Keating was to go after the treasure himself. Devine claimed that Thompson then left St. John's for Ferryland, a community on Newfoundland's Avalon Peninsula. The writer stated that a winter storm had struck that night in the area between St. John's and Ferryland, and Thompson's body was found in the spring on a road near Bay Bulls, twenty-five miles from St. John's, where he was later buried.[7]

The pirate, Captain Marion Thompson, was entertained at Government House (shown here) while he planned his return to the treasure island off the coast of Costa Rica.

6. In regards to the Governor's name in 1840, Devine was incorrect. LeMarchant served as Governor from 1847 to 1852. Sir Henry Prescott was Governor from 1834 to 1841.

7. Neither St. John's or Bay Bulls has any death record of Thompson. The only similar case recorded during that period is that of Thomas Eden, who perished at Bay Bulls on December 31, 1840, and was buried in that community.

Another version of these events claimed that Thompson, while visiting the home of the merchant James Boag, was approached by a prominent city lady with whom he had socialized. She came to Boag's home to warn Thompson, "I don't know what crime you've committed, but they are coming to arrest you." Thompson went to the Keating home, where Keating and Captain Wm. Boag were engaged in conversation. He told them the news he had just heard and drew from under the lining of his coat a parchment map, which he placed upon the table. The map was a chart of a lonely island, with the name Cocos Island written across it. The notation on the map stated that this island was situated about 300 miles from the western shores of South America. The parchment was worn and soiled, as if it had been examined often, and Thompson's hands trembled with excitement. Thompson clutched at the table, and used his fingernails to pry free a splinter of the wood long enough to use as a pointer.

Keating focused his full attention on the splinter as Thompson used it to trace along the map while giving detailed instructions on where to find the hidden treasure:

'You must go to the north-east of the island, and follow the coast line of this bay until you find a creek,' he explained, pressing the sharp point of the splinter into a slight inlet shown on the chart. 'From the high-water mark of this creek you must climb along the bed of the stream, which flows from the inland, measuring seventy paces in a direction west-by-south. You cannot mistake the spot, for, from there, you can see standing clear against the skyline and quite close, a gap in the hills, from anywhere else the gap is invisible. Turn to the north and walk until you cross a stream. You will then see a rock with a smooth face, like a wall, examine it carefully, it rises sheer up like a cliff. But, at the height of a man's shoulder from the ground, you will see a crevice or hole, in which a man might insert his thumb. Thrust an iron bar into that hole, and level outwards, you will then open a cave in which are bars of gold and silver, coins, church images and golden crucifixes.'[8]

The stress was too much for the pirate who had evaded capture for twenty years. When he tried to stand up, he placed his hands on his chest and said, "I'm finished. It's the curse of the Cocos Island Treasure," and fell to the floor. Keating brought in a doctor who lived nearby and he confirmed that Thompson had died of a heart attack.

Regardless of which version is correct, it is certain that Thompson did not leave St. John's on the *Edgecombe* on January 25, 1841, at the start of its adventure to Treasure Island.

The *Edgecombe* set sail from the wharf adjacent to this War Memorial on Water Street, St. John's, Newfoundland, on January 25, 1841.

After giving Thompson a decent burial, Boag and Keating completed arrangements to sail from St. John's on January 25, 1841.[9] My own research into Thompson's death shows that the pirate was in St. John's, in December 1840, preparing for the *Edgecombe's* treasure hunting adventure. While his name does not show up in cemetery records in 1840 and 1841,

8. *On the Track of Treasure*, Herve de Montmorency, 1904.
9. *Doubloons*, Charles H. Driscoll, 1931.

nothing short of death would have caused him to abandon the treasure hunt or to miss the departure of the *Edgecombe* on January 25, 1841. Foul play cannot be ruled out in the disappearance of Thompson while in St. John's.

A possible explanation for Thompson's death that hasn't been mentioned in the records of any of the St. John's churches might be found in the oral tradition in Bay Bulls. When I first researched this story a decade ago, a fisherman named Maloney took me to a small cemetery near the Gun Ridge. He explained that around the mid-nineteenth century, a ship pulled into Bay Bulls near the Gun Ridge and an old pirate was brought to shore and buried at that site. Perhaps Thompson died on the *Edgecombe* and the vessel put in at Bay Bulls to give him a decent burial.

With the cargo of a half load of dried fish stored on board and adequate supplies for the adventure that lay ahead, the *Edgecombe* set sail on January 25, 1841, with a British crew on board. The ship left from the wharf in front of the Customs House (site of today's War Memorial in St. John's, Newfoundland). Fortunately, it was a clear winter's day and the harbour had not yet become blocked with ice. Among those waving farewell from the wharf was Keating's wife Elizabeth and his only child, ten-year-old Margaret.

Courtesy City of St. John's Archives

Barrels of fish at St. John's harbour, waiting to be loaded for shipment to foreign ports.

Keating and Boag had done their best to keep the expedition secret. Not even the crew had been told of the real purpose and destination of the *Edgecombe*. Adding to the secrecy of the adventure was the fact that the brig was to wait at Rio de Janeiro for the arrival of a stranger. Had the weather been favorable, this meeting would have taken place on schedule. The same gale force winds along the coast of South America that slowed the progress of the *Edgecombe* delayed the arrival of the mysterious stranger from Liverpool, England. Finally, after a lapse of six weeks, the weather improved and the vessel from Liverpool arrived.

The long delay in the arrival of the man from Smith & Irwin likely aroused some suspicion among the crew. Why was another person needed? After all, they had a full crew and three Captains on board. Boag and Keating, however, remembered their agreement with Smith & Irwin and knew the purpose of the stranger about to join their expedition. The man, identified in records only as Captain Gault, arrived after the storm had ended and presented his papers to Captains Boag and Keating when he boarded the *Edgecombe*. With the addition of Captain Gault, the *Edgecombe* now had four Captains. The fourth captain, identified in Lloyd's Shipping Records simply as Captain Briz, took charge of the ship from Rio de Janeiro to the Falklands and there transferred to another ship. It wasn't unusual for two or more captains to be on the same ship in those days. Ships' voyages would often be for long periods and would have a series of captains in charge before the ship returned to its home port. Sometimes, captains would simply change ships in a foreign port.

Meanwhile, as far as the citizens of St. John's, Newfoundland were concerned, the *Edgecombe* was on a routine trip to deliver a cargo of fish to Rio de Janeiro. We now know that Boag and Keating had actually agreed to take only half a load of fish from Job Brothers in St. John's to Brazil. This enabled them to conceal the true nature of the adventure taking place, and it also provided them with some extra money towards financing their hunt for treasure. While the St. John's newspapers noted the *Edgecombe's* voyage to Brazil with a cargo of fish, it took a page-by-page review of Lloyd's Shipping Records by this author to confirm the true nature of the *Edgecombe's* mission.

When the *Edgecombe* sailed from Rio de Janeiro, it turned south and headed around the Horn, instead of turning north to return to Newfoundland. Following the Lloyd's records, combined with information from descendants of Captain William Boag, I was able to confirm that the *Edgecombe* stopped over at the Falkland Islands and then went on to arrive at its final destination, Cocos Island — or as it is better known to Robert Louis Stevenson's fans, Treasure Island — on June 18, 1841. When the *Edgecombe* sailed within view of Cocos Island, the first thing the men would have noticed would be the highest peak on the island, Mount Iglesias — sometimes called 'Observation Point' — which would have had a grey cloud surrounding its peak at that time of year. Stevenson's Treasure Island had its own Mount Iglesias. It was called Spy Glass Hill, "...the big one with the clouds on it." June was not an ideal time to recover treasure from the island due to the rainy season having started. It rains on Cocos Island every day from May until November.

Captains Boag and Keating chose to go ashore to scout the area first, while Captain Gault remained on board to control the crew. The two treasure seekers had studied the Thompson map closely and knew the instructions that accompanied it. Having viewed the jungle-covered-island, and experiencing the heavy rainfall, they felt it would be a major challenge to locate the treasure and to remove it from the island — particularly since it reportedly took ten longboats just to bring the Lima part of the treasure trove ashore.

Boag and Keating made their way through the jungle growth and followed Thompson's instructions closely. They were amazed that it had led them so quickly to the treasure cave. Captain Keating estimated the measurements of the

cave to be from twelve to fifteen feet square. Boag was over-
come with the sudden glitter from the treasure and believed
the cave was gleaming with a strange and terrifying light. Once
inside, the two men took account of the mass of wealth. It
contained bars of gold and silver and sacks of coins. The
sacks were stamped with the official mark of the Bank of
Lima and bound up at the mouth with strips of hide. Some
had burst or had worn through, and a stream of gold coins
poured from the canvas.

The treasure contained many beautiful church ornaments,
a number of golden crucifixes and chalices. Among the trove
was a statue of the Madonna in solid gold. This item weighed
750 pounds[10] — so heavy that Keating and Boag together
could not lift it, but could only push it along the floor of the
cave. Once they regained their composure, Keating suggested
that they not tell Gault of their discovery and pretend not to
have found the treasure. The two feared for their lives if the
crew were to witness the size of the treasure. Boag agreed and
they decided to come back later with a crew of men they
could trust and with whom they would share their new-found
wealth.

Boag and Keating filled their pockets with gold coins and
concealed two small sacks of jewels on their persons which
they brought back and hid on the *Edgecombe*.[11] Once back on
the ship, they informed Captain Gault that it would be very
difficult to find the treasure. Gault, seeing the excitement in
their expressions — which they could not conceal — became
convinced that they had indeed found the Lost Treasure of
Lima and were not about to share it.[12] Captain Gault called
the crew together and informed them of the treasure on the
island and shouted, "Lads, we are going to share this stuff
with these fellows!"

10. *On the Track of Treasure,* Herve de Montmorency, 1904.
11. *The Romance of Treasure*, T. C. Bridges, 1931
12. Inspector General Charles Hutchings, Newfoundland Constabulary,
    Newfoundland Quarterly, 1908.

The crew threatened mutiny if the captains refused to give each man an equal share. Keating reminded them that the people who financed the expedition had the right to reap the chief part of the golden harvest and suggested that all the crew members would receive a substantial reward.

This further angered the sailors who shouted, "The stuff is ours and we are going to have it!" Consumed with greed, the crew then went ashore in hopes of finding the treasure.

Keating feared they had a mutiny brewing and reproached Gault for causing the problem. Captain Gault claimed that it was better that the sailors should mutiny before they knew the location of the treasure cave, rather than after the treasure had been brought on board. This was obviously true. The three Captains tried to formulate a plan to avoid a mutiny. When the men returned and demanded to know where the treasure had been buried, Boag convinced them that he and the other captains were willing to share, but in order to do it correctly and guarantee each a fair amount, they would need to go to the British Consul in nearby Panama and draw up an agreement. By this time the men were drunk and, after agreeing to the proposal, soon fell into a deep sleep.

Chapter 3

Keating Finds Lost Treasure of Lima

> Like Oak Island, there are countless legends of vast treasures buried on Cocos Island off the west coast of Central America, and the most outstanding involves a Captain John Keating of St. John's, Newfoundland.
>
> — William J. Crocker, Tracking Treasure — In Search of East Coast Bounty

While in Panama, Captains Boag and Keating, Boag's son — second mate Billy Boag Jr. — and two crew members had been ashore one evening and were returning to the *Edgecombe* by small boat when a sudden squall struck. Their boat was overturned and all of them were dumped into the water. Young Boag, a strong swimmer, headed for shore. Captains Boag and Keating and the two crew members finally managed to cut away the mast and upright the boat. The first mate on the *Edgecombe* heard their cries for help and went to their aid. By the time he arrived on the scene, Captain Boag had disappeared beneath the water and never returned to the surface. The remaining three men were rescued by the first mate, who brought them back to the *Edgecombe*.

Young Boag swam the one mile distance to shore, but was exhausted and almost naked when he emerged from the water. According to the Boag family records, Billy managed to enter town through a broken gate at the end of the main street and hastened as best he could to the residence of the British Consul. A rescue effort was organized by the Consul and they rowed quickly to the area of the accident in a canoe. There was no trace of the small boat or victims, so the canoe continued on to the *Edgecombe*.

Several versions of how Captain William Boag died emerged in later writings on the subject. One of those versions is found in the book *Doubloons* by Charles B. Driscoll. Driscoll mistakenly writes that Boag fell into the water at Cocos Island and drowned after being dragged to the bottom by the weight of gold in his pockets.

The errors in reporting on Boag's death emerged because most writers outside Newfoundland were not aware that young Boag had accompanied his father on the expedition and had returned safely to his home in St. John's, where he preserved the true account of the tragedy.

Inspector General Hutchings wrote that his grandmother, the wife of Captain William Boag, had received a visit from Captain Keating when he returned to Newfoundland from Cocos Island. Hutchings said that Keating admitted his guilt in causing Boag's death to the heartbroken widow and children. The Inspector General explained that Keating begged their forgiveness. Keating claimed what he had done was for the safety of himself and his two comrades. According to Keating, when they got back into the boat, it began taking on water and he pushed Captain Boag back into the water to save himself and his two companions. He described Boag's last minutes: "He went beneath the water and never rose again. He was eaten by sharks."

Jack Fitzgerald researching birth records of Captains Keating and Fitzgerald at the Provincial Archives of Newfoundland and Labrador.

Courtesy Carter-Fitzgerald Black & White Photography

Young Billy Boag later told his family that two days after the tragedy, his father's right arm was picked up on the beach by a gentleman named Collett, who was awaiting the arrival of an English packet with his wife. Captain Boag's arm was buried in a cemetery at Panama City, Panama.

When young Billy Boag returned to the *Edgecombe* the first mate broke the sad news to him of the tragic fate of his father. Another surprise awaited him when he went to his father's cabin. He discovered that his father's sea chest had been broken open and most of the contents stolen. He said that everything of value had been taken, including the charts showing the locality of the treasure cave and the gems and gold his father had brought back to the ship. Young Boag noticed the thief had left behind a small bag in the chest which resembled a button bag. He quickly opened it and saw that it contained some valuable gems. He emptied the bag onto the bed and counted twenty-seven gems.

In 1908 Charles H. Hutchings K. C. — who later became the Inspector General of Police in Newfoundland — published a story in the *Newfoundland Quarterly* about the then famous Cocos Island Treasure and its connection with Newfoundland. In this article, he revealed the amazing family secret that he was the grandson of the Captain William Boag, who died during the 1841 expedition of the *Edgecombe*, and that two of the gems taken from the treasure cave were still in his possession.

His knowledge of the Cocos Island events came from three sources which he listed:

1. Letters from his uncle William Boag Jr. written to his sister, who was Hutching's mother.
2. The extracts taken from the logbook of the *Edgecombe* by his uncle William Boag Jr.
3. The traditions within the Boag family.

Meanwhile, Keating took his belongings and the loot he and Boag had taken from the treasure cave and quietly slipped into Panama. From there he made it overland to the Atlantic coast where he signed on a ship and worked his passage back to Newfoundland. In an account of his adventure, which he wrote in 1878, Keating said:

> In Panama, I hired two mules and a guide to go across the Isthmus. The *Edgecombe,* then in charge of Captain Gault, sailed for the Pearl Islands for a load of shells. I drew a rough sketch of the island (Cocos Island) while there, as there was no chart in my time. I stated where we anchored, and where on Cocos Island treasure was buried. I sold the gold from the treasure in St. John's for 1300 pounds Sterling.

Keating's hiring of two mules suggests that perhaps the treasure he brought back was more considerable than he had later claimed. Some believed that Keating brought back more of the treasure than indicated in several statements made over his lifetime. He likely did not reveal his real take from the Lima Treasure to any person, because Keating was a man who did not trust others. In his book *The Great Treasure Hunts*, Rupert Furneaux speculated that the full value of the treasure recovered in 1841 by Keating was between $7,000 and $110,000. In the book *Doubloons,* Charles Driscoll estimated that Keating brought back $15,000 in gold. At the time Keating brought back treasure, even a few thousand dollars would be a considerable amount. In those days a seaman earned eleven dollars per month, and a judge about seven hundred dollars per year.

Two people who may have helped Keating in converting the gold to money in 1841 and 1845 were a Newfoundland industrialist and politician, Charles Fox Bennett, and a Harbour Grace merchant, Robert Trapnell, whose family later entered the jewellery business in Newfoundland. Trapnell was a close friend of Captain Keating, and served as best man at Keating's second marriage in 1871. The Trapnells of Harbour Grace operated a business importing lumber and exporting fish. Keating had worked for Bennett, both as a captain and as a ships' carpenter. Bennett operated a ship building yard on Water Street in St. John's, Newfoundland, where the Post Office is located today, and a brewery on Sudbury Street. Both properties were leased by Bennett from one Johanna Keating.[1]

Courtesy City of St. John's Archives

The area occupied by the old General Post Office on Water Street, St. John's NL, was once owned by Johanna Keating.

Another interesting aspect of the Keating-Bennett relationship is that when the mail carrier the *Falcon* went aground at Ferryland in 1851, it was Bennett who purchased and salvaged the wreckage. Included among the cargo on that vessel was a quantity of Spanish silver coins dated 1820. They were similar to those said to be included among the stolen Treasure of Lima. Pictures of these same coins have been included in

1. The 1884 Last Will and Testament of Johanna Keating.

Dr. Ina Knobloch's German television documentary on the Treasures at Cocos Island.

The Spanish coins were being mailed from St. John's to Nova Scotia where, in 1845, Keating had a business partner. Could they have been destined for that business partner, a Mr. J. Stewart? Another possibility is that after purchasing some of the Lima Treasure from Keating, Bennett may have sent the coins to a buyer outside Newfoundland. His rush to purchase the wreck of the *Falcon* was suspicious. Whether or not Bennett, or Trapnell, was really involved in purchasing treasure items from Keating may never be known. Some of the coins recovered from the *Falcon* are currently in the possession of the Newfoundland Museum, although nothing but similarity and coincidence can connect them to the stolen treasure of Lima.[2]

Keating returned to Newfoundland from the 1841 treasure-hunting expedition with every intention of going back to recover more wealth from Cocos Island. He shared his secret with very few people, but word soon got around the city that he had found pirate treasure while in South America. The *Edgecombe*, however, did not return to St. John's.

According to Charles Hutchings, the *Edgecombe* was taken over by Captain Gault and remained on the Pacific Coast in 1841 searching for the treasure. Gault died twelve months later at Panama after being poisoned by an insect bite. He was buried at the English Cemetery in Panama City alongside Captain Boag's arm. The *Edgecombe*, having lost both skippers in one year, set sail for Liverpool in August 1842, under the command of Captain Braithwaite, and arrived there on October 22, 1842.[3]

---

2. In Keating's era, Spanish gold doubloons sold in Newfoundland for $15.05 each. This exceeded a seaman's monthly salary by four dollars. A one quarter doubloon sold for $3.80. All Spanish eight gold doubloons sold for $1.90. One Spanish dollar equaled one Newfoundland dollar in 1871. (*Newfoundland Directory*, 1871)

3. Lloyd's Lists, 1840-1844. Between 1843 and 1844 the Edgecombe made several visits to Havana, Cuba. It is not known if these trips had any connection with the recovery of treasure.

Records do not show whether Keating communicated with his English backers, Smith & Irwin. Once back in St. John's he gave little indication that he had benefitted from any treasure hunt. He resumed family life and was employed as a sea captain. In late 1842 he was hired as captain of the *Customer,* which was owned by the Knight Brothers, shipping merchants of St. John's. On October 9, 1844, he took command of the *Atlanta,* owned by the Stewart Company,[4] which had ships in Newfoundland and Nova Scotia. It was while serving on the *Atlanta* that Keating formulated a plan to return for more treasure without having to share it with anyone. He approached John Stewart, a partner in the Stewart Shipping Company, with a proposal for a joint venture to fish for pearls in the South Pacific. Stewart was impressed with the idea and an agreement between the two men was drawn up and signed. Keating had suggested that they purchase a ship at Panama for the project. Unknown to Stewart, Keating had a different venture in mind.

Loading a brig at St. John's harbour during the nineteenth century.

4. Charles Fox Bennett sold the *Atlanta* to Stewart.

Return To Treasure Island

Although Keating wanted all the buried Treasure of Lima for himself and had trusted very few people in St. John's with his secret, rumors of his treasure-seeking adventure had spread and he became known around St. John's as *Keating of the Cocos*, the man who had found a pirate's treasure. His new partnership with Stewart offered him the opportunity for a second secret expedition to recover more of the loot. Early in the year 1845, Keating took his wife Elizabeth and daughter Margaret with him to Nova Scotia. Only Elizabeth and Margaret returned to St. John's on the Stewart-owned vessel, *The North American,* during May 1845.

Captain John Keating left Nova Scotia on one of Stuart's coasting ships for Aspinwall, Panama. There, he purchased a schooner weighing 120 tons and made it clear to those he encountered that he was going pearl fishing. However, the story of the Newfoundlander who had taken treasure from Cocos Island was well known along the Pacific Coast and while Keating was seeking a crew, an unidentified Canadian recognized him as the man who'd found the Lost Treasure of Lima. To the chagrin of Keating, he told the others and soon many men were volunteering to work for the Newfoundlander.

Captain Keating was furious and sought out men who had no knowledge of his background. When his recruiting was complete he set sail to search for pearls with a stop-over at Cocos Island to take on fresh water. His plan was to quietly recover another portion of the treasure to bring back to Newfoundland. Despite his intentions, unfavourable winds and persistent calms delayed the ship and, after fifteen days at sea, Keating was forced to sail into Puenta Arenas, Costa Rica for fresh water and provisions.

In his book *On The Track of Treasure,* Herve de Montmorency commented on the crew's mood:

The motley crew had become very insubordinate, and they were on the verge of mutiny when, as a result of a second attempt, Keating at last reached Cocos Island.

In Keating's statement of 1878 he recorded much of the history of his experiences on the 1845 expedition:[5]

The history of the Cocos Island treasure was so well known on the Pacific Coast that none of the sailors had any doubt as to my reasons for anchoring off the place. One of the crew, a rough old sea-dog of over forty years experience, suddenly remembered in his cups what his memory failed to recall in his soberer moments, that the one man who had ever succeeded in bringing away gold from the Treasure Island was named Keating.

A deputation of sailors (the least drunken of the crew) came aft and asked me point blank if I were not in search of treasure. A dispute followed and one of the mutineers, holding a pistol to my head, demanded that I should take them ashore at once that night and show them the treasure. I managed to pacify the men by giving them more rum. Night was made hideous by songs and drinking and in the morning the whole crew went ashore. I persuaded the men to believe that the treasure was hidden in Wafer Bay and the boats were rowed accordingly to the north-west part of the island where the whole party landed upon the beach. I managed to slip away and swarming up the rocky slopes of the island, was soon lost amongst the thick undergrowth. The mutineers hunted for me for four days, mad with fury at having been baffled. They seized all the liquor on board the schooner and kept up hideous drinking orgies which lasted, without

5. *On the Track of Treasure,* Herve de Montmorency, 1904.

interruption, for twenty-four hours. At the end of this time, they were thoroughly depressed — the stimulating effects of the spirit having worn off, they hoisted anchor and set sail for the mainland, leaving me marooned.

I had brought ashore as much as I could carry from the schooner, and I had a flint and steel and some tinder; with these I was able to light a fire and I continued to support life on eggs and shell-fish. On the third day I was fortunate enough to capture a turtle and this provided me with food for some time. With a needle and thread, I sewed coins, which I recovered from the cave, into my clothes, thus securing gold to the value of about 2800 pounds sterling.

A whaling vessel came into Chatham Bay for water, after I had been eighteen days upon the island. I was becoming very depressed and weak from the want of proper food; indeed, I was quite light-headed, and the crew of the whaler was almost afraid to approach me, for I was raving and shouting. The sailors said that sometimes I appeared to be mad with fury, at other times wild with terror. I was taken on board and a few days later transhipped to a passing vessel bound for Panama.

Keating took a whaling ship from Panama back to Nova Scotia where he caught a freighter coming to St. John's. Once again, it is believed he contacted his sources to exchange the treasure for money. Soon after, word rapidly spread that Captain Keating had been to Cocos Island and had brought back more of the pirate's treasure. People watched his every move. It made him uneasy, suspicious and indecisive. A possible indication that Keating had acquired some wealth was after his return from Cocos Island, his wife became involved in charity work in St. John's.

The Gold-Filled Coffin

Some think Keating had buried some of his Lima loot for safe-keeping. In regard to this there is an interesting story preserved on the province's southern shore. According to the oral history of Renews, sometime around the mid-nineteenth century a boat pulled into the wharf at Renews and sought permission to bury a dead seaman. Permission was granted and a cart was hired to carry the casket to the cemetery. Pall bearers from the ship carried the casket from the ship and placed it on the cart. At the cemetery they removed it and after praying over the grave, filled it in and left.

After the vessel left port, the cart's owner was shocked to notice that the steel rod connecting the cart's wheels had bent from the weight of the coffin. When word of this spread through the community, people speculated that the casket must have been filled with pirates' gold. Several years afterwards, some people decided to solve the mystery and opened the grave to inspect the 'gold casket' as it was called. To the surprise of everyone, the casket was missing and it has been speculated that at some point the pirate ship had returned to recover the treasure.

The story fuels speculation that the ship and gold-filled casket contained the hidden portion of the Lima Treasure taken back to Newfoundland by Captain John Keating

The Gold-Filled Grave

Another story from the oral history of Keating of the Cocos Island involved the popular belief that he had brought back far more of the treasure to Newfoundland than he had ever revealed in his lifetime. Some people speculated that he had hidden some of his treasure at, or near, his family burial plot at Belvedere Cemetery in St. John's.

During filming of the German documentary on the Lima Treasure, producer Dr. Ina Knobloch noticed that a grave near the Keating plot was different than others in the area. At first glance, the difference is not apparent. Like many others in the area, it is surrounded by a wrought iron fence. However, this grave, unlike all the others, did not have a gate, and was completely encircled with black wrought iron palings. Adding to the interest in the gravesite was about eighteen inches of the lower portion of two of the palings had been sawn away.

Dr. Ina Knobloch, producer of the German documentaries on Cocos Island Treasures, and Jack Fitzgerald with television crew at Belvedere Cemetery, St. John's, NL

Captain John Keating lived off his money comfortably for a few years in St. John's, but in 1849, tragedy struck the Keating family. Their only daughter, Margaret, died from tuberculosis in March 1849, and in January 1855, his wife Elizabeth passed away. The two are buried side by side at the Belvedere Cemetery, St. John's, Newfoundland.

John invested his money in a shipping and merchant business in the Port aux Basques area on Newfoundland's west coast. He continued for a few more years to live in his Duckworth Street home, east of the Customs House in St. John's.

One night, alone in his kitchen, he opened a box on his kitchen table and began removing gold pieces and counting them. Unknown to him, a young woman named Elizabeth Woods had stopped to peek in the window. Elizabeth was intrigued by the stories of Captain Keating's adventures to Cocos Island and now saw the evidence of his success for herself.[6]

A romance soon developed between the two, which led to marriage. Since Keating's brothers had moved to the Port aux Basque area to look after Captain John's business, Keating took up residence there as well after marrying Elizabeth. When Elizabeth and some members of her family began pressing him to tell where he found the gold, he suspected that she had married him to find out about the treasure. Just as he had misled others about where on Cocos Island the treasure could be found, he misled his wife. He always told her it was buried in Wafer Bay rather than Chatham Bay, where he had located it.

6. *On the Track of Treasure*, Herve de Montmorency, 1904.

Chapter 4

Enter Captain Nick Fitzgerald

"You have my secret, and I was a fool to give it to you, but if you do not find the cave, no man ever will. You are now the only man alive who can do so."

— Captain John Keating to Captain Nick Fitzgerald at Codroy, Newfoundland, 1868.

Herve de Montmorency, author of *On The Track of Treasure*, published in 1904, told of his adventure to Cocos Island in search of the Lima Treasure. The author had teamed up with retired British Admiral Henry L. Palliser and, in preparation for the expedition, they researched the story of the piracy of the treasure and its subsequent finding by Captain John Keating. Captain Nick Fitzgerald, believed to be the only person whom Keating had trusted with instructions on where to find the treasure, provided the two adventurers with letters outlining the secret in exchange for a share of the loot. The expedition was unsuccessful, but it did discover something that convinced them they were near success. In a river bed they found a silver crucifix which the author felt had been dropped by the pirates bringing the treasure to the Island, or by Keating when he removed part of it.

During late February 1868, the *George T. Fog*, a fishing schooner sailing off the coast of western Newfoundland, was broken by heavy ice and became waterlogged. The owner of the schooner, Captain Nicholas Fitzgerald of Harbour Grace, Newfoundland, was

Courtesy Carter-Fitzgerald Black & White Photography

A silver cross similar to this one was found by treasure hunters on Cocos Island.

aware of the conditions in the villages along the coast and
decided to stay with his vessel as long as he could. Several
other ships were wrecked at the same time and some of the
crews made their way across the ice to the community of
Codroy, near Port aux Basques. Despite the fact that residents
of this community were short on provisions, they welcomed
the shipwrecked sailors. Ice floes coming down from
Labrador had blocked access to western communities by sea
and made it impossible for supply vessels to bring them much
needed provisions.

Fitzgerald was about twenty miles off the coast and managed to man his vessel for almost two weeks. Fortunately, a
barque came by just as Captain Fitzgerald was about to give
orders to abandon ship, and successfully rescued the Captain,
crew, and all their provisions. The barque found an opening in
the ice floes which enabled it to sail straight into Codroy.
Fitzgerald and his crew unloaded their provisions and shared
them with the inhabitants and other shipwrecked sailors.

In his book, Montmorency described how Fitzgerald
came into contact with Captain John Keating. He reported:

> Fitzgerald was generous in distributing food and
> comforts and while going about the place attending to
> the wants of the shipwrecked crews, he came upon a
> broken-down house or shed. The floor was caked
> with ice and the cracks in the roof allowed the wind
> and the snow to drive in. Some of the castaways were
> lying on the ground in a miserable condition. Among
> these was an old man who was enveloped in a piece of
> rough sail canvas; and it appeared he was dying.
> Fitzgerald took pity on him and had him carried to a
> room which he had engaged for himself in the village.
> Puting the stranger in his bed, Fitzgerald attended to
> him and watched over him with such success that he
> brought him through his illness; but while the out-
> come of the stranger's condition was still doubtful,

the stranger vowed that he was not ungrateful.

One day, while Fitzgerald was waiting on him, he said suddenly: 'What are you doing this for? Do you know who I am?'

'I don't know you at all mate,' answered Fitzgerald quietly, 'and I'm not doing anything out of the common, as far as I can see. One doesn't leave a chap to die like a rat in a hole — leastways, I think not!'

The castaway continued earnestly:

'Well, I don't know your name, but I do know you are a humane fellow. I've lived long, and I've never met real kindness before. In return for what you've done for me, I'll put you in the way of becoming a rich man, if you'll accept my offer. I am Keating, the man folks call Keating of the Cocos Island Treasure. It's true that I've been to the island twice and brought treasure away with me. I can go again, and I can take you with me, if I recover. In case I do not, I will give you my secret now. Only you must promise me first that if I live, you will not reveal to anyone what I'm going to tell you, and that you'll go with me to Cocos Island and help me to remove the treasure you shall share.'

The name Keating, and the romance and mystery attached to it, were known to Captain Fitzgerald. The two men drew up a rough agreement which both signed. Captain Keating then told Fitzgerald how he came to meet the pirate of the *Relampago*, and the leader of the mutineers of the *Mary Dear*. He didn't tell his story all at once, but in parts, as his strength permitted. Fitzgerald was shaken when Keating related the circumstances of Boag's death, and he suspected that foul play may have been involved. When Keating recovered, he reminded Fitzgerald of their contract and expressed a wish to begin planning for their expedition to Cocos Island. By this

time Fitzgerald was having second thoughts. Montmorency
described Fitzgerald's thinking:

> The closer his acquaintance with Keating, the less
> inclined was the old sailor to venture on any under-
> taking in which he might share the fate of Captain
> Boag. He was, however, an honest man, and he
> respected his part of the bargain with Keating, which
> compelled him to preserve the latter's secret during
> his lifetime. Keating died in 1882. It was not, there-
> fore, till fourteen years later that the chance publica-
> tion in a Canadian journal of an account of Captain
> Shrapnel's visit to Cocos Island aroused in Fitzgerald's
> mind a wonder whether the knowledge he possessed
> might not prove of use.

Several years later, Montmorency revealed that Shrapnell
was a pseudonym used by Admiral Palliser to avoid undue
public attention. Montmorency observed that:

> The romantic narrative disclosed in Fitzgerald's
> letters given to Palliser formed a fitting sequel to the
> legends of the treasure hidden on Cocos Island by the
> mutineers of the *Mary Dear* or by the pirate Bonito. It
> was clear that the pirate mentioned by Keating in the
> Fitzgerald letters must have been either on board the
> *Relampago* or the *Mary Dear*. Perhaps he had been on
> both vessels, as the name Thompson occurs in the
> records of the trial and execution of the mutineers
> deposited in the national library at Lima, where they
> can be seen to this day, and the same name is found in
> some old letters which tell of Bonito's career. Thus
> Keating's story dovetailed with the Peruvian records
> and the traditions repeated in all Pacific ports suffi-
> ciently to arouse Admiral Palliser's keenest interest.

Although Thompson's name is said to have been mentioned in Lima court records, he was not among those executed.

While statements alleged to have been written by Captain Keating did not identify the person who gave him the treasure map in 1840,[1] descendants of Captain William Boag did identify the stranger as Captain Thompson.

In further correspondence, Fitzgerald explained that Keating had been suspected of the murder of Bogue and that his prosecution had been dropped for lack of sufficient evidence. The ravings of the fever-stricken seaman in the frozen hut in Codroy seemed to reveal the burdened state of Keating's conscience, and it wasn't difficult to suspect the grim significance of his reluctance to revisit the treasure cave alone.

Several years earlier Fitzgerald had written a number of letters to Admiral Curzon-Howe of the Royal Navy, offering to give him the map to the treasure on Cocos Island in return for five percent of the recovered loot. Fitzgerald approached Curzon-Howe because he believed an armed naval vessel would have the best chance for success in recovering the treasure. According to Charles H. Driscoll, Fitzgerald admitted in one of his letters to Curzon-Howe that he had refused to accompany Keating on a contemplated expedition, fearing he might share the fate of Boag, and that this refusal had thrown Keating into a passion. Fitzgerald stated in that letter:

'You have my secret,' the latter had said, 'and I was a fool to give it to you; but if you do not find the cave, no man ever will. You are now the only one alive who can do so!'

He really hissed these words with clenched teeth and I was glad to get away from him.

Keating's feeble brain was saturated with suspicion and dread; he lived in fear of his life, expecting

1. *Doubloons*, Charles H. Driscoll, 1931.

to be murdered when at home, because of the secret
he would not divulge to his relatives.

According to Driscoll, after learning of Keating's death in
1882, Fitzgerald said he visited Keating's family at Sydney,
Cape Breton, to view the charts and plans which they possessed. Keating's widow had married a Mr. Brennan at Cape
Breton, Nova Scotia. It is not clear whether Captain Keating
had been living in Cape Breton at the time of his death. Cape
Breton is closer to the Codroy-Port aux Basques area, where
Keating operated a business, than it is to St. John's, and would
have been convenient for business purposes. After viewing
the documents, Fitzgerald considered Keating's family of no
help because Keating had misled them into believing the
treasure was buried at Wafer Bay.

Fitzgerald was assisted in writing his earlier letters to
Admiral Curzon-Howe, and later letters to Palliser, by a close
friend and neighbour at Harbour Grace, who was also a
school teacher in that community.

Other information forthcoming from Captain Fitzgerald
was that Keating's second wife spent her life trying to worm
the secret of the treasure out of him. Captain Keating left a
death-bed statement and a chart with his wife, but according
to Fitzgerald, neither appeared to be genuine.

The Death-Bed Statement
August 6, 1882

On the map you will find marked No. 1 which
means a cave. It is positioned off the ground and not
down in the ground. It is on the surface. The grass
grows high on this level, when you are at it you cannot see it. I was there a good while before I found it.
My back was resting against the stone that formed the
door. I took away the stone, and removed 1300
pounds Sterling, which I concealed in my clothes. I

replaced the stone in its original place as I had found it. I left it just the same as I did four years earlier. There was no person with me at the time. I left the vessel this day alone, and I returned to the vessel, no person knew that I had found the money, if they did my life would have been in great danger. They said that they would take my life if I did not share the treasure equally with them. When I heard this it put me on guard so I kept all a secret.

On No. 2 marked on the map, a place called Morgan's Point, are $5,000,000 worth buried. By the side of the river in Anchorage Bay are three pots of gold coin. I could not bring it to bear to go back a third time.

This is my last and full statement, so help me God.
Sgd. John Keating
Witness: Matthew Hendrikson and Captain John Phillips

The death-bed statement referred to Keating's second trip made in 1845 to recover treasure at Cocos Island. A paragraph had been inserted into the statement in different handwriting than Keating's that read, "My wife is not to show this paper to anyone without first receiving one hundred pounds."

The chart of the island in Keating's widow's possession was a wretched scrawl with the instructions:

Go round Morgan's Point — Morgan's Point corresponds to Cascara Island in the Admiralty Chart — into Wafer Bay keep on the north side until you are hid from the open water.[2]

While there is doubt regarding the information contained in this document, the two witnesses mentioned in it were neighbours of Keating while he lived in St. John's. When

2. *Doubloons*, Charles H. Driscoll, 1931.

Keating's death notice appeared in St. John's newspapers, it did not mention the place where he had died.

Fitzgerald asserted that Keating's death-bed statement contained false clues which Keating left to mislead his wife, and that Keating had gone to his grave having shared his secret only with him (Captain Fitzgerald). Keating, according to Fitzgerald, had destroyed the parchment chart given to him by Thompson in 1840. The old sea-dog had planned on a third trip to the Island in 1880 with a boyhood friend from Harbour Grace, Captain William Hackett. Unfortunately, Hackett died on a trip to the West Indies and Keating's health began to fail.[3]

In the late 1890's, Brennan and Hackett led one of the most unusual expeditions ever to seek the treasure on Cocos Island. Following Keating's death in 1882, there was competition between his widow and stepson-in-law, Richard Young, to put together an expedition to find the Lima Treasure. Captain William Hackett had told Admiral Palliser that Keating had assured him he had given Young accurate instructions on finding the treasure. Hackett's son, who was employed as a factory worker in St. John's, Newfoundland, was to join Young on an expedition to Cocos Island; however, they were unable to raise the necessary funds.

Keating's widow soon became Mrs. Brennan, and began her own plans to find the treasure. She formed a partnership with Captain Hackett's brother Fred, and together they organized their own expedition. To discourage others from investing with Richard Young, the couple put an advertisement in a Sydney, Nova Scotia newspaper, which records identify as the *Newfoundland Sydney Herald* (sic). The advertisement quoted Captain Keating as stating that he had not given the treasure map to Richard Young, and stating, "I have given to Thomas Hackett all the papers and all the information that I ever possessed necessary to find the treasure buried on Cocos Island."

3. *Doubloons*, Charles H. Driscoll, 1931.

Among Captain William Hackett's belongings were papers relating to the treasure given to him by Keating. These papers were given to his brother, Captain Fred Hackett, who was living in Vancouver. After Keating's death, Hackett's brother had shown an interest in searching for the treasure. Mrs. Brennan approached Captain Hackett and they put together a team of six rowdy and rough ex-sea captains for their expedition. The Aurora Expedition, as it was called, suffered great hardships. They had a small vessel and it took forty-three days to reach Cocos Island from Vancouver.[4]

Montmorency described their behaviour on Cocos Island. He said:

> They were a rough lot, and when they found nothing, in a fury of disappointment, they stripped the old woman and searched her clothes, and broke open boxes. They were convinced that she possessed some information which she was holding back. Mrs. Brennan, who was bent double with age, contrived to climb to the top of the high ground above Wafer Bay, where she stood contemplating the outlook.
>
> 'This is not the place, boys,' she kept repeating, 'it ought to be a bay with a small beach shaped like a crescent, with black rocks on either side, where you are hid from the open water.'
>
> Hackett would not listen to her and, when she protested that the men were not working in the right spot, retorted, 'Shut up, you old fool, you know nothing!'

On the return trip, the Aurora Expedition ran short of provisions, and the adventurers nearly starved.

4. *The Book of Buried Treasure*, Ralph D. Paine, 1922; *Dig for Pirates Gold*, Robert Nesmith, 1958; and *Doubloons*, Charles H. Driscoll, 1931.

Meanwhile, in 1897-1898, the retired British Admiral Henry L. Palliser carried out extensive research into Captain Nick Fitzgerald's background. He learned that Fitzgerald was well known and respected throughout Newfoundland and had friends in powerful positions there, including a judge of the Supreme Court of Newfoundland. Palliser put a series of key questions to Fitzgerald to satisfy himself of the veracity of his information. The admiral concluded that Fitzgerald was a credible source.

However, before mailing his papers to Palliser, Fitzgerald obtained an agreement that the ex-naval officer would not reveal the secret of the clue to the treasure cave to anyone except those going on the expedition with him. Palliser also had to guarantee that Fitzgerald would receive five percent of whatever might be found. With this agreement in place, Captain Fitzgerald mailed letters to Palliser on May 23, 1898, giving him the precise information needed to find the Lima Treasure. He informed Palliser that a great surprise awaited him if he found the cave. He wrote:

> The cave, if found without the door being damaged or blown up, will surprise all who see it on account of the ingenious contrivance and workmanship, possibly done by Peruvian workers in stone, whose skill was noted. In Keating's words, the cave is between twelve and fifteen feet square, with sufficient standing room. The entrance to it is closed by a stone made to move around in such a peculiar manner that it sets into the rock when you turn it, leaving a passage through which one man can crawl into the cave at a time, when the stone is turned back in its place, the human eye cannot detect it; it fits like a paper on a wall. You have to find a hole into which a man's thumb can fit when you find that mark, insert into it an iron bar. One man can easily turn it.

In that cave are gold and silver and images enough to load a vessel. I have thought this matter over for years, and decided that a man-o'-war was the only safe way to secure the treasure — that it would be best protected under our national flag. I was afraid to write to the commanding officers of the Navy, fearing that they would laugh at my romantic story; until one day I heard the petty officers of Captain Watt extolling him for his kindly disposition. I then took courage and wrote to him. He has not moved in the matter, but he gave me his word that he would keep my secret. Keating told me that the first time he went to the island he had no trouble in finding the cave, but the second time, there had been a disturbance or eruption which changed the features of the place, but he found it all the same. I beg to state that I thought I had the whole thing well committed to memory, until I began to write to Captain Watt, and discovered I had forgotten the exact number of paces told to me by Keating — that is, from the last bearing. However, I am confident that it is either seventy or one hundred and seventy paces, and this would not be much for sailors with jack-knives to search.[5]

Admiral Palliser's communications with Captain Fitzgerald in 1896 stemmed from efforts by Fitzgerald to interest a senior British Naval Officer in an expedition to search for the Lost Treasure of Lima. The following letter to Commodore Curzon-Howe was located and published by Charles Driscoll in his 1936 book *Doubloons*. Nick Fitzgerald sought out Curzon-Howe, because the Commodore, while serving in the area of Newfoundland, once had saved his life.

5. *Doubloons*, Charles H. Driscoll, 1931; *The Book of Buried Tresure*, Ralph D. Paine, 1922.

Harbour Grace, Nfld.
September 10, 1894

To the Hon. Commodore Curzon-Howe

Dear Sir,

    I presume to address you in what may appear to be a very strange and romantic subject. I believe there is a treasure lying concealed in the Cocos Island, Pacific Ocean. I believe that I am the only person who knows the secret where it lies. Now as you are occasionally on duty in the Pacific and as a warship is the most suitable means of carrying out such a project, I thought that it would be to my advantage to write to you, and explain the facts of the matter to you.

    How I came to the knowledge of this secret: in 1868 fortune had thrown me as a shipwreck sailor from a sealing vessel on the shores of Codroy village on the west side of Newfoundland, and there I met the owner of another schooner that had been lost in the ice at the same time that we were. This man's name was Keating, a native of this country, and generally known at least by the old inhabitants of St. John's as the man who was on two occasions fitted out with vessel and crew to bring the treasure that still remains hidden, in a very secure way, at Cocos Island.

    When I met Keating in 1868, he was in great distress. I had the power to assist him, which I did, bringing him to my lodgings and my own bed, caring for him in his sickness. In return for acts of help on my part he entrusted to me the secret of where the treasure lies hidden at the Cocos Island. We drew up an agreement, one of the conditions being that I should go with him for the treasure, another condition was that I should enter the cave alone as he had pledged himself never again to enter it. (I attribute that to fear of something.)[6]

However, the agreement was not carried out because I, having a family to see to and believing that Captain Boag, the only man who had the secret from Keating at the time, had mysteriously disappeared in his company while at the Cocos Island, I thought I would be running grave risk of my life to go single-handed with him. This disappearance of Boag was unsatisfactorily explained to me by him.

Therefore, I believe that I alone possess the secret of where the treasure lies hidden at Cocos Island. I am the only person who can find or show how it may be found. The condition that I will disclose the secret is this:

That you will send me an agreement signed by you, sir, that if you or any person acting for you, or any way on account of this information, get the treasure you will hand over to me one-twentieth part of the gross value of what is in the cave. The treasure comprises gold coin, silver coin, gold images of the Madonna, life-size church images.

If you desire any further information on this matter I shall be only too happy to supply it to you or any question you may be pleased to put.

Yours respectfully,
Nick Fitzgerald

Curzon-Howe passed the letter to Palliser, who did collect a great deal of additional information from Fitzgerald before setting out with Montmorency for the Cocos Island.

---

6. In the nineteenth century, treasure found in the form of gold coins was generally melted and sold secretly as boullion in an effort to cover up a treasure find. Today, gold doubloons are worth many times their weight in gold.

In his book *The Great Treasure Hunts*, Rupert Furneaux observed:

> Fitzgerald could hardly have invented his description of the cave and its door, which sounds like something lifted from King Solomon's Mines, in which Rider Haggard described a massive stone that rose and descended to open and block the treasure chamber. Such, however, must have been the description given to Fitzgerald by Keating, whatever he told Hackett and his wife. It appears to have been an entirely different explanation, for nowhere else in the legend does the story of the door appear.

According to Fitzgerald, the reason for the failure of so many expeditions arose clearly from the fact that they landed and searched in Wafer Bay; whereas the treasure was carried in boatloads to a certain creek in Chatham Bay — a creek which can be identified by Fitzgerald's clue. After searching for the treasure twice, Palliser concluded:

> The search was hopeless; landslides, previous excavations, and the torrential rains of this tropical region had so entirely altered the face of the island that clues and directions were of little avail.[7] Meanwhile, the bearings and diggings of disappointed searchers in Wafer Bay must remain for all time monuments of their vain pursuit of wealth.[8]

Palliser set out to make enquiries and gather evidence from other sources, in anticipation of another expedition.

An interesting assessment of the clues provided in the Fitzgerald-Keating papers to the treasure was made in 1927 by

---

7. *The Book of Buried Treasure*, Ralph D. Paine
8. *On the Track of Treasure*, Herve de Montmorency, 1904.

Captain Anthony Mangel after searching unsuccessfully for the treasure that year. He used a version of the Keating-Fitzgerald instructions obtained from the Nautical and Traveller's Club at Sydney, Australia. Mangel concluded that the papers referred to Wafer Bay. In this, he was mistaken because the authentic Keating-Fitzgerald instructions applied to Chatham Bay and not Wafer Bay. Regardless, he came to an intriguing conclusion. His party located a cave with its entrance below water. This place was not mentioned in the Fitzgerald-Keating papers which stated:

> Disembark in the Bay of Hope between two islets in water five fathoms deep. Walk 360 paces along the course of the stream, then turn NNE for 850 yards, stake, setting sun casts the silhouette of an eagle with wings spread at the extremity of sun and shadow; cave marked with a cross. Here lies the treasure.

Mangel concluded that the direction to the treasure was flawed due to changes over the years in how measurements were made. He explained:

> We were now in the twentieth century, and there-fore working with a sextant and other accurate instruments which took into account the declination of the compass. Thompson on the other hand had hidden his treasure in 1820 (sic), and had worked out the spot with an octant.

Mangel felt Thompson's calculations, as described in the Fitzgerald-Keating papers, needed to be redetermined repeating the same mistakes, and using data from the nautical tables of the period.

The treasure hunter adjusted the Thompson calculations, and corrected the bearings to latitude 5° 10' 17" and 87° 0' 40" longitude. He succeeded in finding a cave south of the Bay of

Hope, on the south coast of the island, and NNE of Meule Island. The entrance to the cave was only accessible for about one hour at low tide. He rowed his dinghy into the cave, and while probing the sand felt a resistance which he believed might be the treasure. When the tide began rising the sand was washed back into the cave, and he was lucky to escape. He managed to get out just as the tide filled and then buried the cave. Mangel did not continue his search.[9]

Captain Nicholas Fitzgerald was likely the only person to whom Keating gave a truthful account of how and where he found the treasure. Like Captain John Keating, Fitzgerald's name plays a prominent role in the history of the Cocos Island and the Lost Treasure of Lima. At the time this book was written, his name is better known outside Newfoundland than in the province. Most books written about the Treasures on Cocos Island include the name of Captain Nicholas Fitzgerald. All books on the same subject mention Captain John Keating as the man who found the Lost Treasure, and sparked over four hundred expeditions to Cocos Island. The whereabouts of the Fitzgerald documents after his death in 1906 is not known. It appears that Keating did give misleading information to his friend Captain Thomas Hackett, similar to that given to his wife.

Captain Nick Fitzgerald's death notice was carried in the *Evening Telegram* on May 31, 1906, the same day he died. The message was telegraphed to the city and published the same day because of Fitzgerald's prominence in Newfoundland. It read:

Nicholas Fitzgerald died this morning at 6:00 a.m. after ten days illness. He was 68 years old, and carried on the fishery business the greater part of his life. His death was due to bronchitis. He left a wife, a son and three daughters.

9. *The Romance of Buried Treasure,* T.C. Bridges, 1931.

Captain Fitzgerald was better known inside Newfoundland as a successful fishing captain whose views on the resource were often sought and welcomed by authorities. *The Evening Telegram* of June 1, 1906, praised Fitzgerald:

> In the death of Nicholas Fitzgerald, Harbour Grace loses one of its most prominent citizens, and the country a man of wide knowledge and extensive experience in the staple industry of our province home. At an early age he took up seafaring life, and for many years followed deep sea voyages sailing out of this port (St. John's) and Harbour Grace.
>
> Having tired of seafaring life, he settled down in the prosecution of the fishery. He devoted special attention to the herring industry in which he was the most successful of any who followed this industry on the Labrador. Here for years he advanced a better cure, and publicly expressed his opinion that more attention to the curing and packaging of our herring would make it a profitable industry.

Chapter 5

Clues to the Treasure

Levering the log out of position, he released the accumulated pool of water which left the area dry. In the midst of this he had caught sight of a glittering object, this, when drawn out, proved to be a portion of a crucifix which might once have adorned a Peruvian church.

— Herve de Montmorency, On the Track of Treasure, 1904.

Not since 1841 when Keating and Boag slipped out of St. John's Harbour in a successful hunt for the Lost Treasure of Lima, had any leaders of a treasure hunting expedition possessed so much confidence and optimism over the outcome of their endeavour as did Herve de Montmorency and Admiral Palliser. Montmorency and Palliser[1] had done their homework. The two had collected all available background to the treasure and its hiding place. Among their research was information from three sources which they felt had a direct bearing on the location where the treasure had been buried.

Preparations for the expedition involved obtaining Captain Nicholas Fitzgerald's papers. Fitzgerald was the only person with whom Keating is alleged to have shared his secret. They also had Chapelle's map which had emerged in California in the 1840's and was believed to be reliable because he was with Thompson when the treasure was stolen and later buried.

A third source was the instructions obtained from a man named Flower, who was not actually searching for the treasure. Palliser obtained Flower's clue from a Mr. Alexander in Buenos Aires, who was employed as a station master at San Patricio Station, on the Buenos Aires and Pacific Railway. Alexander often discussed the possibilities of finding the Lima Treasure on Cocos Island with his shipmate, Bob Flower. In his younger days, Flower served as an officer on a steamer which, on several occasions, was used for expeditions

---

1. In Montmorency's book *On the Track of Treasure,* the author, at the request of Palliser, changed Palliser's name to Shrapnell. In 1936, the author disclosed that Captain Shrapnell was the name used by British ex-naval Admiral Palliser.. Subsequent authors have used the Shrapnell name.

to Cocos Island. Alexander related the following story to Palliser:

On his last visit to the island, which was in 1875, he was with a rough group of adventurers. While he was walking on high ground above a creek, he slipped and fell about fifteen feet down a bank which ran into a stream. When he got back on his feet, he noticed a pile of stones heaped in pyramid form in front of what he described as "a fox-hole." He cleared the stones and entered the cave. Inside, he found piles of gold ingots and kegs of coins. Flower removed as much as he could carry and replaced the rocks as he had found them. He used his watch to determine the bearings of the cave. The stream below him lay to the south, and thirty fathoms or so from there the brook ran into the sea in a direction east-northeast from the mouth of the river; the eastern point of Chatham Bay bore due east.[2]

Bob Flower was drowned several years later in a wreck of one of the steamers owned by the Pacific Steam Navigation Company. Palliser said that Mr. Alexander's integrity was vouched for by his employers, and Alexander claimed he had seen the coins found by Flower.

Montmorency and Palliser made an unsuccessful effort in South America to hire a suitable vessel to take them to Cocos Island. Finally, they came up with a creative way to get a ship for the expedition. They made a deal with the owners of a vessel called the *Lytton,* which was scheduled to carry a cargo of cement from England to a Mexican port on the Pacific side of that country. The adventurers made a deal to lease the vessel for one month after it had completed its delivery. The owners saw this as an opportunity to reduce its shipping expenses, because shipping costs for cement were high. A deal was consummated, but Montmorency and party were required to find their own way to Salina Cruz on the Mexican Pacific Coast to join up with the *Lytton.*

2. *On the Track of Treasure*, Herve de Montmorency, 1904.

The line of succession of those believed to have inherited the true directions to the Lost Treasure of Lima starts with Captain John Keating, who received them from the man who stole the treasure, Captain Marion Thompson. Keating was said to have passed on the secrets to his second wife, Elizabeth Brennan, and his friend Captain William Hackett, but it seems that he may have deliberately given them wrong information. Keating may have shared the true map and directions only with Captain Nick Fitzgerald of Harbour Grace, who shared the secret with Admiral Curzon-Howe, Admiral Palliser, and Herve de Montmorency.

The following description of the Montmorency and Palliser Expedition's search for the Lima Treasure in 1903 is based on a collection of information gathered from many sources, but primarily the following books: *On the Trail of Treasure; Great Treasure Hunts; The Book of Buried Treasure,* and *Lost Treasures.*

Three days after the *Lytton* had left Salina Cruz, Montmorency, who had religiously protected the research on the treasure's location, laid before the assembled conclave of buccaneers all the clues that he and Palliser had collected. The expedition's leader itemized and explained each one to the assembled members of his party. He said:

1. Fitzgerald's (Keating's) clue — From the mouth of a creek in the N.E. Bay seventy paces west by south; then walk to the north until a rock like a cliff is seen.
2. Chapelle's clue — From a sand stone boulder in the south-east of the bay, between a conical rock and an islet which looks like a squatting lion; 140 fathoms north-west-by-west, thirty-five fathoms west-by-south, eighty feet north, and thirty feet from a black-faced crag.
3. Flower's clue (measured backwards) — True west from Pitt Head lies the mouth of a creek;

west-south-west thirty fathoms from the sea, and face
to the north.

Enthusiasm among the group heightened when it was
pointed out that if all lines were traced upon the chart of
Chatham Bay, in accordance with these instructions, they will
converge to almost the same spot. When it is remembered
that the three sources of information were independent of
one another, the sanguine hopes of the adventurers may be
excused.

Being a practical person, Montmorency figured out that
the reputed treasure, valued at twelve million dollars, would
form a bulky mass weighing over sixteen tons, having the
capacity of thirty-two or thirty-three cubic feet. He anticipated finding a large cave. The expedition leader pointed out:

> Repeated warnings had reached us that we should
> be molested on arriving at Cocos Island. Those of our
> party who had chosen the New York route to Mexico
> had received on their arrival in America two cables
> from England warning them that we should find an
> expedition on the island prepared to contest our
> advance. It was decided, therefore, to give Wafer Bay
> a wide berth and to arrive at Chatham Bay under
> cover of darkness. The high ground in the north of
> the island would prevent anyone in Wafer Bay from
> being aware of our presence when we had cast
> anchor.

The ship approached Cocos Island on Sunday, August 9,
at 4:00 a.m., with every crew member on deck to witness their
arrival. It was still dark and misty, and by 5:00 a.m., the first
shouts of 'Land Ahoy!' were heard as a dull mass of land
began emerging from the mist. With the rising sun the land
turned from grey to purple, from purple to green, and at last
the moment for which they had long waited had arrived. It

was Cocos Island with its lofty peak, abrupt cliff-like shores, and thick tropical vegetation, displaying its beauty to the admiring eyes of the adventurers. Admiral Palliser described the view that greeted him as he arrived on shore:

> So thick are the trees that from a small distance they appear like moss upon a stone, while here and there cascades of fresh water shoot off the high ground from amongst the undergrowth right into the sea, falling from a height of over a hundred feet.

When the *Lytton* dropped anchor into thirty fathoms of crystal clear water, the splash startled flocks of birds that suddenly went screaming from the land and circled the vessel overhead to the delight of the adventurers. The men tried to identify the birds. There were boobie birds, gannets, gulls, small dove-like birds with webbed feet, frigate-birds with wings stretched stiff like the sails of clipper.

Cocos Island is a typical home for the frigate-bird, for she is indeed a pirate, soaring aloft and awaiting a chance to seize from some smaller member of the feathered tribe its hard-earned proceeds from a morning's fishing.

Montmorency described the waters beneath the surface at Cocos Island:

> We could see the strangest, the most beautiful fish, darting by the thousands from the dark caverns of coral and sponge. Dull green sharks, with impertinent tameness, poked their snouts inquisitively at the *Lytton's* sides, as though challenging us to offer them a meal. Now and again a giant skate, as big as two ordinary blankets, and more evil in appearance than the sharks, would flap for a minute on the surface of the bay.

The adventurers got a glimpse of a geographical point often described by those who participated in earlier expeditions. Breakfast Island located on the northern end of Cocos Island and viewed from a westerly direction strongly resembles a sphinx. The treasure seekers measured the depth of the waters between Breakfast Island and the large rock in a small islet off the north-east point as thirty fathoms. Chatham Bay ran in through this channel, narrowing itself into a sandy creek between the two rocks. Far out to sea is another rock, marked in some charts as 'the Boat.' In the early morning the adventurers were convinced this was a ship, but the rising sun dispelled the illusion.

The band of impatient treasure seekers was ready to make their first landing on Treasure Island at 8:00 a.m. that morning. With expectations running high, the men boarded a longboat and rowed towards the end of the Bay. Montmorency recalled:

> We all worked while astonished birds, so unaccustomed to man as to be fearless, wheeled screaming around our heads, or actually perched on the handles of the oars. We had gone hardly halfway when someone called out, "Why, we are thirteen!" Including 'Man Friday' we were thirteen. Then like a flash, all the bad omens which had shown themselves since our departure passed through our minds. The changing of our ship's name from the *Scotia* to the *Lytton*; the disappearance of the black cat on board *La Normandie*, and the shooting of a pelican by one of our party. But if buccaneers be superstitious, they have neither long memories nor low spirits and as the keel grated upon the coral and sand of the shore, we vaulted over the gunwale of the cutter and waded or were carried to the beach, as merry as crickets.
>
> The sandy beach where we landed was strewn with enormous boulders, and on each was carved the

name and business of a vessel which had visited
Chatham Bay. Some of the dates carry one back to
Nelson's days, and men-o'-war, whalers, and pirates
alike, appear to have made this deserted spot a water-
ing place. The high watermark is sharply defined by
the cessation of growing shrubs and trees and by a
line of rotting vegetation cast up by the rising tide
with a northeasterly wind. The spray must splash the
leaves of the coconut palms which nodded solemnly
to us, perhaps in welcome, perhaps in mockery.

The pelican of the wilderness was cooling herself
in the surf, within five yards of our boat as we landed;
undisturbed by our appearance, she bobbed up and
down in the breakers, spreading her wings and puffing
out her feathers for all the world as does any old
'Martha' of the bathing machines at Margate, whose
skirts, when she wades out to sea, are inflated like a
balloon. Within ten minutes of our setting foot on
shore, 'Man Friday' had pitched our tent and spread
out our stores and instruments. While this was being
done the others were busy climbing trees and smash-
ing open coconuts.[3]

Palliser had
carefully studied
all the clues
which had
brought them to
the northeast of
Cocos Island
and he began
outlining a plan

Montmorency and Palliser on Cocos Island

to follow the instructions step by step. In order to confirm
they had landed in the right spot, he told the men they should
look for a creek. "From the creek," he said, "flowed a stream

3. The direct quotes used from page 2 to this page are taken from *On the Track of Treasure*,
Herve de Montmorency, 1904.

of freshwater from the southwest which passed through a gorge about two hundred yards from its mouth." The instructions directed them to find the high-water-mark and they used a pocket compass to measure seventy paces in the direction west-by-south.

The gorge was not visible from the sea. From just about every position on the beach there was no evidence to suggest there was a gorge in the area. The instructions were to find the gorge and count seventy paces from the mark of a high tide. From there they would have to take a fresh bearing due north and to walk until they crossed a stream. At this position a bare-faced cliff-like rock would become visible, in which would be the treasure cave. This could be opened by inserting a crowbar in a crevice and levering the stone outwards.

Montmorency took a close look around the landing area and began to doubt they were in the right place. He considered that because so many people had visited and searched the area, someone would have very surely discovered the treasure. After sharing his views with Palliser, they decided to search the whole of Chatham Bay. They spread out and began cutting and hacking with their bill-hooks to clear a passage through the thick jungle undergrowth which was as tough and impenetrable as a wire entanglement.

The expedition members faced a daunting challenge in making their way inland. Cutting through the thick jungle appeared to be impossible, so they chose to find a stream and follow its course. This required wading through shallow waters, climbing over slippery boulders and jumping from one boulder to another in parts where the river flowed through deep pools. They found encouragement from their collection of clues which showed that once they were on the right track, the treasure would be simple to find. Palliser concluded that the pirates would have opted to bury the treasure near the sea rather than try to carry it over and through such rough and treacherous terrain.[4]

4. *The Book of Buried Treasure,* Ralph D. Paine, 1922

It didn't take long for the treasure hunters to find a brook flowing from the hills which had worn a valley to the sea. Their starting point began at the mouth of the creek, formed by the outlet of the stream of fresh water. They climbed along the bed of this little river and searched inland, but failed to find the gorge or rocky formation mentioned among the clues. At this point Montmorency noted that, judging by the features of the ground, it did not appear that the area described by Keating would be found at this location. He commented, "One might as well expect to find a field of barley in the midst of Piccadilly."

The area was covered in a rich red soil and a tangle of creepers and bushes. In the bed of the stream were pebbles and slippery boulders. While struggling to cross the brook, a member of the party fell into the water when the rotten log he was using as a bridge broke. Immediately the others showed concern for his safety and began making their way to his assistance, when they were reassured by the victim's shout of, "Why didn't you 'Kodak' me?"

About half an hour into their trek a member of the team noticed something unusual beneath the water. He stopped to investigate and suddenly became very excited. He signaled to the others and shouted, "Come on, I hardly dare say so, but I believe I have found something."

The rest of the team made an effort to conceal their excitement until they had a chance to inspect the discovery. When they arrived on the scene, their friend was lying on his stomach with his face in the water, peering under a great rock which half covered the entrance to a small cave. Each member of the team took a turn at inspecting the find. They unanimously agreed that there were sacks stored about ten to twelve feet inside the cave. The question to be answered now was, could this be the treasure cave mentioned by Captain John Keating?

Palliser dampened their enthusiasm with his comment, "If they be sacks, it is certainly not the treasure; for sacks would have rotted years ago."

Another buccaneer, mopping his brow and panting, wondered aloud if anyone could have hauled treasure up that rough path, or dragged himself there by night in the darkness.

Montmorency took a second look and declared he had little doubt that the white masses dimly visible in the cave under the shadow of the overhanging rock were canvas sacks. The seam of one sack could even be distinguished, while the corner of the nearest one was wrinkled and folded over in the most natural fashion. The team considered which person among them would be the first to enter the cave. There was little enthusiasm towards being the first because of the fear of snakes and reptiles that inhabited the Island. The least that they expected was a thorough soaking in mud and the bite or sting of some insect.

Palliser observed, "The best goods are made up in little parcels," and suggested that the smallest man in the group be given the honour of first entering the cave.

The smallest man agreed to take on the job and managed to insert himself into the darkened cave. He returned smothered in mud with a disgusted expression. "No," he said, "they are only lumps of clay but I could have sworn they were sacks until I touched them."[5]

A lengthy debate among the team followed this disappointment. Palliser suggested continuing up the stream, but the rest were very much against this course. Montmorency pointed out that they had wandered far beyond the measurements as given by the clue and that the winding of the brook had carried them outside the compass-bearings. An agreement was reached to continue for another few hundred yards. This move also ended in failure and they returned to the seashore. Once again they searched for the treasure. The

5. The direct quotes used on this page are taken from *On the Track of Treasure*, Herve de Montmorency, 1904.

group followed the highwater mark, striking inland when possible. They were confronted with a series of rocks rising perpendicular from the sea, all of which restricted their movement in all directions.

The expedition team stopped at a fresh water pool for a lunch of sardines and biscuits and amused themselves by spelling the quaint carvings on surrounding boulders. This was followed by bathing in the pool, after which they watched swarms of crabs scuttling across sand and rocks to get to the sea. By afternoon they were ready to resume their search for the treasure. Thick jungle growth covered the area and possibly concealed some of the clues mentioned by Keating. The group laboured to cut away the growth and even removed some of the soil. At 3:00 p.m., the skies opened up and a downfall of rain drenched the men, forcing them to abandon the hunt and return to their ship. The day's work had ended in failure and a mood of discouragement prevailed.

Not only had they suffered through hours of hard labour in tropical heat, and a thorough drenching from the heavy rainfall, but an army of red ants suddenly swarmed the beach and attacked them. They arrived on ship wet, fatigued, and covered from head to toe in ant bites. Palliser was convinced that the clues they had spent so much time gathering were insufficient.

Montmorency observed that the extraordinary richness of the tropical vegetation and the network of fresh streams continually carrying earth and debris from the steep interior hills over a sixty-year period must have altered the area beyond recognition.

The following day the rain continued. By 10:00 a.m., when there was no sign that the rain would cease, they decided to ignore the discomforts of a drenching and headed out to search Chatham Bay. Every moment on the Island was important to their search and they unanimously had agreed to continue the hunt for the Lima Treasure. However, this time they took a different approach and relied less on the instructions and clues they had collected. They rowed a boat from the north end of the Island to the eastern point and, with the aid of bearings and measurements, examined every landing spot in that part of Cocos Island.

Montmorency wrote, "We thought that, by having done this, we should have exhausted all possibilities."

Both the sphinx and the mainland presented an awesome view from the deck of the *Lytton,* which was moored in the channel between them. The surf breaking against their steep shores over the years had worn enormous caves into the rocks. The caverns were so vast that the Island seemed to be supported upon archways. Adding to this beauty were the colorful trees growing from the crevices in the steep cliffs that served as a roosting place for the wide variety of birds on Cocos Island.

The adventurers had little time to bask in the beauty of the Island because they were well aware that beneath this panoramic display of nature lay hidden dangers. Hundreds of penguins perched along the rocks peering down on the *Lytton,* like spectators in a Colosseum watching in expectation of the unavoidable tragedy that lay ahead.

Montmorency and Palliser assessed the situation and concluded that landing on this part of the Island would be utterly impossible, for the shore could be as vertical and slippery as an iceberg. In his writings, Montmorency noted:

> It is dangerous to approach the cliffs in a boat since the breakers, on the calmest day, lash themselves into a foam as white as snow upon rocks as sharp as needles.

The two expedition leaders led the party from the north point towards the lower end of Chatham Bay, searching for places where Keating might have landed in his successful search for the treasure cave. The team passed several indentations — but all agreed these could hardly be called creeks —

in the coastline. None of these sites were practical landing
places at a high tide. They felt that one part was accessible
only by wading — almost swimming — to reach the shore at
a low tide.

No doubt the landscape had undergone changes since
Keating's first visit in 1840. One small bay had been filled
entirely, perhaps by an earthquake that caused an overhanging
cliff to break off, sending tons of boulders and clay into the
sea. Rowing beyond this point they followed the coast which
runs abruptly southwest at near right angles to the general line
of Chatham Bay forming a creek — overshadowed on the
right of a boat rowing towards shore by a cliff-like rock.

The treasure seekers found that all along this great wall
runs a ledge, possibly cut by man, and used for a landing stage.
The site at low tide served the party well, but at high tide it
was difficult to access. At high tide they had to maneuver
around boulders using a boat hook, then beach the boat upon
the site and wade ashore.

The depth of the stream was unpredictable. In some
places the water was shallow enough to walk through without
footwear getting a complete soaking. Other parts gurgled and
bubbled into great black pools ten to twelve feet in depth. For
a hundred yards or more they clambered the water course; but
so thick and high was the undergrowth, and so steep were the
banks, that it was hardly possible to observe the general features of the land.

Trees and boulders swept down by floods and torrents
created a series of effectual dams throughout the length of
the river. The struggle along the river was a real challenge. The
undergrowth was so thick and high that the men found it
nearly impossible to observe the general features of the land.
The physical effort of the day exhausted the men and the
search was called to a halt. While returning to the beach a
member of the party, attempting to find a foothold, stumbled
over a fallen tree and fell head over heels into an old river bed,
which some tremendous landslide must have forced from its

original course. Getting back on his feet the enraged buccaneer, while rubbing the bruises on his knees, noticed the precise form of rocky foundation they had been searching for.
Stepping back towards the stream he turned his eyes to the
southwest, and to his delight, saw a great cleft in the hills as
though it was cut by a canon, through which a river flowed
from inland.

The find generated a mild burst of enthusiasm among the
searchers and some of them continued their hike towards the
beach. Measuring the length of the cleft accurately was not
possible due to the roughness of the ground, but those who
remained estimated it at seventy yards, while the bearing from
the mouth of the creek was exactly west-by-south.

From the spot where the gorge was visible they took a
second bearing and advanced due north. In this attempt they
were not so fortunate. The ground was simply a network of
streams and it was immediately evident that there had been
considerable disturbance of the land recently. The treasure
seekers were puzzled when confronted by a bank as they
advanced, but they were not deterred and continued clearing
the undergrowth for several acres until they found a reef of
rock, some thirty yards long, protruding at a height of five or
six feet from the ground. The party examined the place carefully, hacked away the vegetation and used their picks to break
the face of the stone.

Palliser and Montmorency made a careful study of their
measurements and bearings and concluded they had found
the place indicated among clues given by Captain Nick
Fitzgerald. They also agreed that the immense amount of soil
swept down the valley by the stream had altered the appearance of the ground. They sought to confirm their finding by
cross-checking it with the information from Flower.

Montmorency commented on Flower's accidental slipping
and falling into the treasure cave, saying:

This was nothing improbable; we buccaneers were continually falling; no living thing can walk on Cocos Island without risking his neck — except perhaps the wild pigs, which are as sure-footed as goats. Many times did they terrify us, as we clung to the ledge of a precipice by our eyelids. Leaping from some thicket, they would dash past us with tremendous bounds, like some red and hairy avalanche.

Trying to find the stream referred to by Flower wasn't easy. Following the instructions contained in their log-book, they measured off thirty fathoms, which brought the party to a broken area of ground and found what they thought was the barefaced rock mentioned in Fitzgerald's clue. At least the exercise of a very small measure of imagination made the distance sixty yards. However, owing to the change in the watercourses it was impossible to identify the stream mentioned by Flower. Palliser observed:

> The knowledge that Flower could not have gone for a walk with a log line in his pocket was flattering unction for our souls. From the mouth of the stream, Pitt Head, the east-by-north magnetic, but it certainly is not east-north-east; so that bearing was found to be some fifteen degrees in excess of our hopes. We again soothed our disappointment with the thought that a bearing taken by the watch is never accurate. There was still time before sunset to test our place by Chapelle's clue; so we decided to walk along the beach and hunt for the sandstone boulder. In the south-east corner of Chatham Bay boulders by scores greet the eye. Yet none seemed very conspicuous. So we went on board disheartened, hungry, and drenched to the skin.

Early next morning Montmorency and Palliser were on deck at dawn. In his diary Montmorency noted:

> The weather next day, Tuesday, August 11, was a vast improvement. The scene from the deck of the *Lytton* was breathtaking. The sun was rising over clear skies. The impenetrable rain clouds of the previous day had vanished as if by magic and the imposing peak of Mount Iglesias could be seen sharp and clear against the sky. On our starboard quarter lay Nuez or Breakfast Island. It has been explained how this rock resembles a Sphinx — the squatting lion of Chapelle's clue. To our port side was a conical rock, looking as though it had toppled over from the steep cliffs of Pitt Head; thus, there could be no doubt we were in the right bay. To confirm us in our opinion, we observed a tunnel worn by the action of the waves through the rocky headland which faces Breakfast Island, through which at low tide (when no swell is setting in from the northward) a boat may be rowed.[6]

In his book *The Great Treasure Hunts*, Rupert Furneaux claimed that Palliser, in his research of the treasure on Cocos Island, obtained an important clue from the Swedish Captain Lars Peter Lund, who visited the Island in search of the gold. Furneaux said that Lund had claimed to have discovered the log of the *Relampago*, Bonito's boat on which Thompson and Chapelle were crew members before venturing out on their own. The log stated that the *Relampago* had anchored in a bay between a cone-shaped rock and a small inlet which looked like a squatting lion. The directions given in the log read:

> A large sandstone boulder in the south-west of the bay; 140 fathoms north-west; thirty-five fathoms west by south, eighty feet north, and thirty feet from the black crag.

6. Direct quotes from *On the Track of Treasure*, Herve de Montmorency, 1904.

The treasure hunters felt they had found the tunnel near where the *Relampago* had lost her anchor. At an early hour, two enthusiastic buccaneers started in the dinghy and rowed from the treasure creek round Chatham Bay following the coastline as far as the most eastern point of the island. It was impossible to land at any place. Indeed, except where two or three streams emptied themselves into the sea, the shore could not be approached without danger, for reefs of coral rose to within a few inches of the surface, threatening with their sharp edges to rip open the bottom of a boat. Heavy weights could only have been landed at the point where the men had first beached the cutter. In the area of treasure creek they found it necessary to wade ashore. Yet, what pirate ever minded wetting his boots?

Palliser made an interesting discovery while wandering the beach at low tide. He found a large rock or boulder, which had many strange marks etched into it. Among others were 'Charles B' and 'West XX North' carved in clearly distinctive characters. He suggested the latter inscription might have meant west, twenty degrees north if the two crosses were intended for Roman numbers. The find raised the spirits of the men of the *Lytton*. The adventurers were delighted when they observed that the treasure creek, found on the following day, bore nearly west-north-west from the boulder. Less satisfactory, however, was the measurement of one hundred and forty fathoms. The mouth of the creek, which seemed to satisfy Fitzgerald's clue, lay some seven hundred feet from the boulder; whereas the full one hundred and forty fathoms carried the end of their measuring line to an impassable precipice.

A lengthy meeting among the treasure seekers was held on the *Lytton* that night after dinner. At this meeting, Palliser expressed the opinion the search was hopeless because of the changes in the features of the land which had taken place over the sixty years since Keating found the treasure. It was determined, however, to make some excavations in the creek where the gap in the hills indicated it could be in the area of the treasure trove.

The conversation changed to the topic of sailing ships. The mate of the *Lytton* described the old method of heaving the load with the knots on the line paid out freely while the sands of a half-minute glass were running.

"Sometimes we used a twenty-eight-seconds glass," said the mate; "sometimes a thirty-seconds glass."

"That must have involved a complicated calculation," remarked a buccaneer, "I mean, using a twenty-eight-seconds glass."

"Not at all," said the mate, "we reckoned it half a minute, and placed the knots on the line closer together!"

"That means," continued our friend, "that a fathom was not always six feet in length."

"Of course not," pursued the mate. "In the old ships, where a twenty-eight-seconds glass was used, the fathoms on the log-line were only five feet in length, or five feet and an inch or two."

This conversation was cheering to the buccaneers, who would then and there have gone ashore to re-measure the distance from the boulder to the creek, had it not been pitch dark. That morning the distance had been estimated at about seven hundred and five feet, which is only seven feet less than one hundred and forty fathoms of five feet one inch each. Montmorency wrote:

We were soon of opinion that the pirates had a twenty-eight-seconds glass for the log-heaving; and by the time that we had all turned in for the night, some of us in hammocks on deck, some of us in our stuffy cabins, most of the treasure-seekers had a hazy sort of idea that no pirate ever was allowed to possess a thirty-seconds glass. More flattering unction!

On the following day the buccaneers, to a man, were ashore by 6:30 a.m., re-measuring their distances and relaying their bearings. The measuring and compass bearings had to be readjusted to conform with their new approach. Additional helpers were recruited from among the crew of the *Lytton*. These men were given shovels, picks, and machetes to clear the soil and undergrowth from the slope where the treasure seekers expected to find the entrance to the cave.[7]

By the sixteenth of August considerable work had been done. Several trenches had been dug from the edge of the stream towards the reef of a rock which they believed was the bare-faced rock of Fitzgerald's clue. However, the hard work brought further disappointment. They found nothing but boulders and red soil piled on the slope to the north of the stream.

At this point the expedition party was running out of time. Only sixteen days were left in their lease of the *Lytton*. This allowed little more than the time needed for the vessel to return to drop them off at Panama and return to their work at Salina Cruz. If the ship was not back at Santa Cruz in sixteen days, an additional fifteen hundred pounds would be owing to the owners. That night Montmorency, Palliser and all members of the expedition carefully reviewed their clues and concluded that no other place on the Island could fulfill the conditions of the clues. They unanimously decided to abandon the hunt and avoid the extra costs which would be incurred by continuing.

The next day was a day of rest and recreation for the expedition party. Some went ashore, and others remained on the boat to try their hand at catching sharks. The ship was not equipped with shark hunting gear, so the men had to impro-

7. Direct quotes from *On the Track of Treasure*, Herve de Montmorency, 1931.

vise to make a proper rod and line. They removed a meat hook from the galley, in addition to a length of steel wire, and a coil of rope. They were surprised to learn that the sharks had no appetite for salt pork which they simply sniffed and swam away. However, when beef was used it was a different story. The sharks went wild for it and fought each other for a choice piece. Montmorency described the sport:

> It was a wonderful sight to see a ten-foot fish, with a hook embedded in his jaw, shaking the bait, as a terrier shakes a rat, twisting and leaping out of the water, his belly gleaming silver-white in the sunshine. We killed seven of the monsters, and had we been provided with barbed hooks, we could have taken seventy. The first shark which we dragged on board bit and snapped and showed signs of life long after the sailors had hacked him to pieces, his vitality being extraordinary. Another magnificent specimen slipped off the hook while being hauled up the side of the ship. As he fell back into the sea, we poured bullets into him from our revolvers and rifles and he turned over and over, lashing the water into foam. Again and again he flung himself into the air, his whole length clear of the surface. The blood from his wounds attracted his comrades and, with savage fury, they dashed at him, tearing him to pieces and playing tug-o'-war with strips of his flesh. So absorbed were we in our fascinating sport, that we had forgotten our friends on shore until the reports of a volley of revolver-shots from the land called our attention to them.

The buccaneers were lined up on the beach, gesticulating and waving to those on board. The adventurers sensed something exciting had been found on land. They quickly launched the cutter and in less than twenty minutes were vaulting over the gunwale and wading ashore. As the cutter neared shore they noticed that one of the men on shore was holding something in his hand. "We have found a piece of silver!" the man was shouting. This news shocked the others who, by this time, were wading ashore. Sure enough, it was a piece of silver; the broken arm of a cross of some church ornament, as far as could be judged.

The man had left the others who were hunting a wild pig for dinner. His persistence led him back to the stream to hunt for the treasure. He waded upstream through the gorge that ran past the banks of clay piled up by the land slips. This buccaneer found the decaying trunk of a tree which had fallen across the watercourse and had effectually dammed the stream. Levering the log out of position, he released the accumulated pool of water which left the area dry. In the midst of this he had caught sight of a glittering object. When drawn out, this proved to be a portion of a crucifix which might once have adorned the altar of a Peruvian church.

The discovery renewed enthusiasm among the expedition party members and they wasted little time in gathering their picks, shovels, and crowbars — ready to flatten the whole mountain if necessary. They first searched the area where the silver cross had been found and could find no additional clues. Palliser suggested that the cross may have washed down from a higher part of the stream. He said that the men crawled along the bed of the stream on hands and knees, finding nothing but a sheet of corrugated iron nailed to a length of timber. They believed this was the remains of a hut put up by Gissler (a German adventurer who spent many years on the island and was given the title Governor of Cocos Island by the Government of Costa Rica), or it might have been left there by the crew of the *Blakeley* (the *Blakeley* expedition was a year earlier). In any case it meant that someone had been in the creek before.

According to an account of the cruise of the *Blakeley*, that expedition took a gold-finding apparatus with them, and, though most of their search was conducted in Wafer Bay, it was recorded that once when they operated with the machine in Chatham Bay, the indications of gold were so strong that they spent hours digging at a spot where the instrument had detected the presence of precious metal. If this story was true, the rains and tropical growth of one summer had been sufficient to obliterate all traces of their work. The Montmorency team cleared the ground of the creepers and undergrowth, uprooting the stumps and detaching heavy rocks, with no success.

They toiled all that day and part of the next morning. Exhausted and demoralized they held a midday meeting and agreed to advise the *Lytton's* captain to weigh anchor and sail for Panama. Montmorency noted:

> Again our windlass stood in the way for departure. In an excess of caution, the anchor had been dropped in nearly forty fathoms of water; our navigator having mistrusted the Admiralty chart, and having been somewhat too self-reliant to care to accept instructions from a naval officer who, on a former visit to Cocos, had anchored his battleship a half-mile nearer the shore.
>
> All this length of cable was too heavy a task for our poor windlass, but our last anchor was at the bottom of Chatham Bay, so it was of vital importance to recover it. While the first mate, with many tackles, wire hawsers, and other lifting contrivances, commenced a ten hours job, some of us went ashore to shoot a wild pig, and others turned their attention to shark fishing. The cunning and skill of the first mate were too much for the anchor; and so, on the nineteenth of August, we steamed out of Chatham Bay. With a view to paying a visit to Wafer Bay, our course was set round the north point of the island, where the great Sphinx rock keeps guard over the treasure — wherever it may be.

As the *Lytton* steamed slowly westward, the treasure seekers marveled at the beauty of Wafer Bay. Opposite Cascara Island, a great cascade 500 feet in height tumbles over the cliff. At the foot of this waterfall is a lovely grove of coconut palms, and trees of great height with red and golden orchids entwined in their branches. The cascade roars and boils into a great basin of rock, which has been worn so smooth by the action of the water that its sides are like polished marble.

When the *Lytton* rounded the point, and the whole of Wafer Bay came into view, the men watching from the ship could see people moving about on the beach in front of corrugated iron huts, which could be seen from behind the trees of the plantation. Montmorency and Palliser decided to take some men and row ashore to see what was happening. Near shore they observed the Costa Rican colors fluttering up a flagpole in the centre of the little settlement. By this time a man had waded out into the water and gave directions with his arms for them to keep to the southern shore of the bay, where a strong stream of fresh water finds its way into the sea.

One of the buccaneers vaulted over the side of the gig as soon as her keel grated upon the sand and, wading forward, the water nearly up to the tops of his sea-boots, grasped the hand of a tall man, whose long beard flowed below his waist.

"My name is Gissler," said the stranger. "I suppose you have come to look for treasure!"[8]

Montmorency conferred with Palliser and they decided that they would stay another few days and search Wafer Bay. To avoid paying late charges to the *Lytton* owners they reminded the ship's captain that he had broken their contract by not picking them up on schedule at Santa Cruz, leaving his company open to a large law suit. In return for not pursuing this legal action, the captain agreed to delay departure for a few more days.

8. *On the Track of Treasure*, Herve de Montmorency, 1904

Chapter 6

Stevenson's Ben Gun

There were traces of their (pirate) old camps, with thirty-two stone steps leading to a cave, old fire-places, rusty pots and arms and empty bottles to mark the scene of their carousing. Gissler (Ben Gun) found some gold coins in this area.

— Ralph D. Paine, The Book of Buried Treasure, 1922

Robert Louis Stevenson's character Ben Gun, in *Treasure Island*, is believed to have been inspired by the German-born hermit of Cocos Island, Augustus Gissler. Gissler had spent more than twenty years living on the island in search of the Lost Treasure of Lima. During his years there Gissler attempted unsuccessfully to colonize it. He did marry, and with the help of his wife, they farmed the land to support themselves. Author Herve de Montmorency encountered Gissler during his visits to Cocos Island in the late 1890s and got to know him quite well. In his description of Gissler the author wrote:

> Having run away from his comfortable home in Germany as an improvident, venturesome youth, he cannot bear to return as a failure to his own country.

Gissler began his life of adventure as an able-bodied seaman on a sailing vessel. Prior to this his only experience in a boat was as a passenger crossing the English Channel. The captain of the sailing vessel was a true bully and made Gissler's sea experience an ordeal. On one occasion he ordered Gissler aloft to loosen the mainsail during a period of high winds. The captain watched as Gissler completed his task and made his way back to the deck. He waited until Gissler arrived on deck to order him back up to secure the gaskets. He did this twice — ignoring the fact that it was obviously making Gissler sick. The experience however, may have helped prepare Gissler for the challenges he later faced while living on Cocos Island.

On a trip from London to Hawaii, Gissler first heard of the treasures buried on Cocos Island. He befriended a Portuguese seaman, Manoel Cabral, who told a fascinating tale of his grandfather's escapades as a pirate with the notorious Captain Benito 'Bloody Sword' Bonito. The seaman claimed his grandfather served with Benito Bonito on the *Rosario*, and also on the *Relampago* (the former *Lightning*) when the pirate captain transferred command. He said that when the *Relampago* was captured, some of the crew joined with Bonito and took the piratical oath.

Cabral Sr. had left written instructions to his family which stated that the *Relampago* be anchored in a bay in fourteen fathoms of water, close to a conical rock that resembled a farmer's haystack. The seaman told Gissler the treasure which was stolen from Spanish priests was very large, and the pirates had buried it on an Island named "La Palma." Cabral said:

> The captain, Cabral and five men carried part of the treasure ashore and walked up a stream until they reached a waterfall that fell from a height of 300 feet, and which they had spotted from the ship. Close by was a grove of coconut trees and in it Don Pedro (Bonito's alias) and Cabral buried the treasure, each taking exact bearings of its position. The hole was dug about twenty feet behind the grove, and about 600 feet west by south from the mouth of the stream.
>
> Don Pedro and Cabral returned to the ship for the rest of the treasure which they carried to the same coconut grove. This time the captain led the way across a small rivulet which they followed for eighty-five feet to a small hill at the foot of which stood a boulder. Cabral dug a hole four feet deep, they placed the treasure in it and rolled the boulder on top. Using the hammer and chisel he had brought, Don Pedro cut on the boulder the letters, D. P. I. 600P.[1]

1. *The Great Treasure Hunts,* Rupert Furneaux, 1931; On the Track of Treasure, Herve de Montmorency, 1904

According to the story, when the *Relampago* sailed to the mainland, Cabral went ashore with others, became involved in a tavern brawl and was injured. Consequently, he was separated from the others. When he recovered and sought to join the *Relampago*, it had gone. He returned home to the Azores and later died on the island of Miguel. A year or so after hiding his treasure, Bonito and his crew were captured by the British. Bonito shot himself rather than be taken prisoner.

Gissler was skeptical of the story. Some time passed, and he heard another tale of pirate treasure very similar to the story told to him by Manoel Cabral. During a visit to Hawaii by Gissler, he played pool with a man named Bartells. When the topic of conversation turned to pirate treasures, Bartells told him that his father-in-law, called 'Old Mac', knew of a deserted island off the coast of South America on which the pirate Captain Benito Bonito had buried a great treasure.

Bartells told Gissler that all Bonito's pirates had been hanged except two men, Thompson and Chapelle. He gave no details as to why these two had escaped the hangman, however this has been explained in an earlier chapter. Gissler thought this would have been a detail known only by the two who had escaped — Thompson and Chapelle. He compared the Cabral and Bartells stories and concluded there was a treasure, and the island referred to as 'La Palma' was the Cocos Island. Gissler and Bartells agreed to go to Cocos Island to search for the loot. This expedition took place in 1888.

In his book, *The Great Treasure Hunts*, Rupert Furneaux stated:

> Bartells produced his late father-in-law's map of an island having two bays on its northeast and northwest coasts. To east and west arose two distinct peaks, and from them two lines were drawn which intersected at a point where a large square had been drawn. The directions, which were written in Spanish, read:

"This island lies in latitude N.5 deg. 27 min. longitude W. 87 deg. It is a healthy place. In the year 1821 we buried here a treasure of immense value. After we had buried the treasure we planted a coconut tree on top and took bearings by compass which showed locations to be N. E. by E. ½ E. to east mountain and N. 10 deg. east to west mountain."

Cocos Island lies at latitude 5º 32' 57" N. And longitude 87º 21' 10" W. And there are two bays at its northeastern and northwestern ends, Chatham Bay and Wafer Bay. Bartells said Old Mac had stated that the treasure had been buried eight feet deep under a high bluff.

Following the failure to find the loot using Bartell's clues, Gissler compared Bartell's directions with those he had obtained from Francisco Maria Jeminez, an official of the Costa Rican Government. From this effort he drew a different interpretation of the Bartell information. Both charts were similar but slightly different in the starting points. He calculated that the line N. 20 degrees West was taken from the inner point of Nuez Island while the other line North 63 East was taken from the Conic Island.

Gissler noted, "As we could now see the (Bartell) plan was not correct because the lines crossed on the gravel beach about twenty feet seaward from high water, whereas by taking the inside point of the Nuez Island we should come to about fifty feet inland from high water." Furneaux commented:

It is at this point, in the year 1888, that the several different traditions relating to treasures concealed on Cocos Island begin to merge; the story received from 'Thompson' by Keating, and that told to Gissler by Bartells, whose father-in-law may have been either Thompson or Chapelle of the *Relampago*. In addition

Gissler now knew of the Bonito treasure in the concealment of which Cabral had participated.

It is more likely that Cabral Sr. and Old Mac were pirates who served under Bonito and had left him before he was captured. This would account for their knowledge of Bonito's hidden treasure and not the Thompson treasure. Thompson, however, had knowledge of both treasures and passed information on the two treasures to Keating.

This was the start of several different versions relating to treasure hidden on Cocos Island. One derived from Captain John Keating himself, who actually found the treasure. Another was told to Gissler by Bartells and likely referred to a separate treasure hidden by Bonito. Gissler and Bartell failed to find any treasure. Bartells, disappointed by the failure, returned to Hawaii and was not heard from again. Gissler continued his search.

In his 1904 book *On The Track of Treasure*, Herve de Montmorency related information he obtained directly from Gissler during the author's 1902 expedition to Cocos Island. Referring to Gissler and Bartell's arrival at Puentarenas, he wrote:

> On the first day after their arrival, they were sitting in the hotel near the beach, when they were accosted by two Englishmen, who begged for employment.
> "Where have you been?" asked Gissler.
> "On an expedition," replied the strangers.
> "What, smuggling?"
> "No, worse than that; treasure hunting on Cocos Island!"
> This strange coincidence appears to have been an important factor in binding the Governor of Cocos

(Gissler) to his task, and bound he is by as strong fetters as hold any galley slave.

Drink of the Nile water, and you will drink of it again. He has returned again and again, fascinated by the fatal spell. Gissler, who, with his strong will and many abilities, might have attained almost any success in life, is still today seeking for the robbed treasures of Mexico and Peru.

The many expeditions which have been to Cocos Island, in search of treasure, have treated him with scant courtesy; his plants have been uprooted, his home has been desecrated, and his stock destroyed; so there is little wonder he looks with eyes of suspicion on visitors to his land.

Once, a British man-o'-war landed sixty marines who threatened his wife and tore up his crops during his absence, while they were excavating the side of a hill in search of gold. How we gained his confidence would take much patience to tell, and perhaps more patience to understand; nevertheless, we did so, and he told us the tale of his life for sixteen years on the island.

Emerson says that no nation can be great which has not stood in the jaws of need; and, so it may be with individuals. On the first occasion when this modern Robinson Crusoe arrived at Cocos Island with his friend, the 'Boatswain' he had neither food nor shelter from the rain. While his gun remained serviceable, he was able to secure an occasional pig, but unfortunately the spring of his Winchester became damaged, and so he was dependent on his dog for hunting. By-and-by, his faithful hound was killed by a boar; then he was reduced to knocking down seabirds with a stick in order to procure food; and, on these, crayfish, and berries he and his comrade, 'the Boatswain', contrived to keep alive.

The 'Boatswain' lies buried on the bold headland in Chatham Bay, which throws its shadow in the afternoon across the stream which we had christened Treasure Creek at the sanguine beginning of our search.

By 1902, the most informed man alive on the treasure hidden at Cocos Island was Augustus Gissler. He collected every piece of evidence and sifted through it with patience and care. Gissler was convinced that with the necessary capital he could recover the treasure. Montmorency concluded:

No man can find the treasure, even with Gissler's aid, who is not prepared to devote at least one year of his life to working on Cocos Island. There is something correct in all the clues; but there is always something missing.

During his years on the Island, the old hermit had learned much of its secrets and history. He confided to Montmorency the tale of Bonito's treasure on the island, and a secret connected with it. Later recalling Gissler's story, Montmorency noted:

'The *Relampago* anchored off the tunnel in the rock' — so says Gissler's information   'and while several boatloads of treasure were being rowed ashore, she lost her anchor in the foul ground and drifted on the tide round the north point near Breakfast Island. Those unloading the treasure on the beach immediately returned to the boats, hurriedly replacing the treasure and rowing after their ship. The dread of being marooned was ever present in the thoughts of the pirates and once aboard again, the crew set to work to make sail, putting enough canvas on her to give their vessel steerage way. Then they lay-to off the rough coast between Wafer and Chatham

Bays. There is no anchorage for a ship, but a boat can be rowed ashore and protected from the heavy rollers by a line of detached rocks. Material can with safety be disembarked on the shingle.' (Shingle refers to a rocky part of the beach that extends out into the water like a peninsula.)

The Hermit

The Bonito treasure has often been confused with the treasure stolen by Captain Thompson. Thompson had been a crew member on the *Relampago* when Bonito buried treasure on Cocos Island which was taken from Peruvian churches and a Spanish Galleon. It was later, after Bonito had died, that Thompson stole the Lima Treasure and added it to the trove on Cocos Island. Montmorency revealed more of the secrets Gissler shared. He wrote:

> The pirates rowed the treasure ashore in eleven (sic) boatloads at high tide; they dropped their precious cargo into the sea, inside the line of breakers, and, landing, waited for the tide to fall — for at low tide the shore cannot be approached, owing to the coral reefs. The gold and valuables were then hauled

to the foot of a cliff which rises abruptly from the beach like a wall; a 'Spanish Burton' (pulley-system to move heavy weights) was rigged by the aid of a hold-fast, made by chiseling a hole in the rock and sinking an eye-bolt into it at the crest of the cliff. Thus the treasure was hoisted up and deposited on a ledge.

The land rises somewhat gradually for thirty or forty yards beyond the crest towards a ridge of rock. Behind this ridge is an open space or hollow, some two acres in extent, on which a few trees are growing. The treasure was further whipped up this slope and over the ridge by a running tackle, and the precious store, having been thrown into a natural hole or crack in the ground, was covered up by the pirates with earth and stones.

To one of the buccaneers, Gissler confided this story of an agreement having been signed between them, binding them, binding our friend, never to work for treasure without the permission of the Governor of Cocos Island. On the following day, the two went overland to the spot, cutting their way through the undergrowth and clambering over the rough ground for six hours in preference to rowing for half an hour, for fear of divulging the secret to the boat's crew.

After gaining the trust of Gissler and accompanying him to the described treasure site, Montmorency was encouraged by what he witnessed. He described the scene:

The rusty eye bolts are still in the rocks which formed the hold-fasts for the tackles; and, amidst the tangle of undergrowth, can still be seen rusty iron pots, a broken sword and the breast-bone of a man. From the ledge to which the treasure was first hoisted our 'treasure seeker' contemplated the bay; on the right was Nuez Island, a squatting lion, to the left a conical rock; north-west-by-west of him lay a sandstone boulder, whose base was just washed by the tide commencing to flow; from behind him, a stream of water poured down the slope and tumbled over the cliff in a cataract to the sea.

In his book *The Romance of Buried Treasure*, author T. C. Bridges revealed that Gissler told the treasure seekers he had found additional evidence of the presence of pirates in the area. The hermit had found many traces of the pirates, including old cooking pots, rusty muskets and empty bottles.

Author Ralph D. Paine disclosed in his book, *The Book of Buried Treasure*, that Gissler found other evidence of a pirate presence. He noted:

> There were traces of their (pirates) old camps, with thirty-two stone steps leading to a cave, old fireplaces, rusty pots and arms, and empty bottles to mark the scene of their carousing. Gissler found some gold coins in this area.

Charles H. Driscoll claimed that Gissler, for all his effort, had uncovered only one gold coin, a Spanish Doubloon dated 1788. However, prior to his death in New York on August 8, 1935, Gissler revealed that he knew where the treasure was hidden, but would not reveal the location, nor start his dig because he wanted to negotiate a better deal for himself with the Costa Rican Government. In the area where the treasure was hidden, he said he had found thirty-three gold coins, minted in 1773 and 1799.[2]

The Montmorency party remained at Wafer Bay for three days after being entrusted with the secret clue. During this time they enjoyed bathing and fishing in the creek behind the settlement.

2. *The Great Treasure Hunt,* Rupert Furneaux, 1931.

During the twenty years Gissler spent on the Island he had constructed living quarters that included a farming area. At one time, he had even brought settlers from Germany to develop the island. The settlers left after a few years, leaving only Gissler and his wife on the island.

Members of the Montmorency expedition had developed a deep respect for Gissler, who was given the title of Governor of Cocos Island and awarded a small salary by the Government of Costa Rica. Montmorency wrote:

> The Costa Rican Government promised to send their one steamer once in every six months to visit the island, but their one steamer is in repair and due to the revolutions is never serviceable when a promise has to be kept. In the old days of sailing vessels, ships frequently called for water, but nowadays steamers never approach the place.

Gissler would not sanction excavations being made at the possible treasure site, which he had located, by any party unprepared to carry the work through to the end. Montmorency had concluded that this would involve a six months task, and consequently, any further search for treasure by them was out of the question. Montmorency recorded in his journal:

> August Gissler, with his wife and a peon, had gone eighteen months without seeing a fellow creature; and, had not curiosity prompted us to visit Wafer Bay before sailing for Panama, he might have remained for eighteen years in his lonely home without setting eyes on a human face. The monarch of all he surveys is Governor Gissler; and he has made for himself fairly comfortable quarters. He has captured some of the wild pigs and domesticated them; and he owns a horse, a mule and a bull. Some years ago, he brought

livestock to the island; but the goats uprooted his plantations, doing more harm than good, and the *Blakeley* expedition[3], with heartless selfishness, slaughtered his three cows. Taking advantage of the fertile soil of Cocos Island, this latter-day Robinson Crusoe has cultivated every sort of vegetable and fruit which the tropics produce.

He grew coffee in the uplands and in the valleys grew tobacco, cocoa, manioca, vines, sweet potatoes, limes, oranges, bananas and pineapples. When the Montmorency expedition arrived, Gissler had been out of flour for more than three months and survived strictly on produce he had cultivated on the island.

By all counts, Gissler was a resourceful and intelligent person who managed to turn all the products of Cocos Islands to his uses. The rubber plant, the iron-wood, and a particularly useful tree, the bombax fera, supplied him with many useful substances. Using the fibre of the bombax fera he made brushes, brooms and ropes, and from its juice he procured tannic acid and ink.[4]

Gissler was able to tan pigs hides to make leather for the repair of his boots, or he could write the records of his life with a quill plucked from the wing of a frigate bird, independent of cobblers and stationers alike. Montmorency noted:

> Gissler was never in want of oil, for coconuts abound on the island, and from these he extracts sufficient to furnish him with light. On two occasions, this remarkable man has built himself from the timbers of trees which he has felled a boat in which to sail to the mainland, her sails improvised from the sheets of his bed, and her ropes woven from the fibers of

3. The *Blakely* expedition took place in 1902 and was under the command of Captain Hackett, who had gone there several years earlier with the widow of Captain John Keating.

4. *The Great Treasure Hunts*, Rupert Furneaux, 1931.

banana trees. Gissler, used his homemade boat to pick up supplies and conduct personal business at Costa Rica.

It is impossible to think of the courageous adventurer upon his frail bark, fighting the elements night after night — his fingers cramped upon the tiller and his eyes straining to pierce the darkness — without feeling the romance of his career. The grip of his strong hand, and the sharp, suspicious glance from his deep-set eyes, reveal at once his determination, and his independence.

Gissler took the Montmorency party on a tour of the island. He showed them the water wheel which he constructed to drive his sawmill during his first days on Cocos Island when he was ship building. According to Montmorency they were taken through the dense, tropical forest where the birds were so tame they would flutter around a person's head and peck at his hat. He described small birds, coal-black in colour, and yellow birds resembling canaries in plumage and in song. The tamest birds, the adventurer said, were the white birds with webbed feet and which the sailors called the Holy Ghost birds because they would drop down from the skies and settle on the hat of anyone moving in the forest. Montmorency noted in his journal:

It was on the twenty-third of August, 1903, that we heaved up our anchor and said a final goodbye to the most romantic spot in the world, Cocos Island. Gissler, his wife and his peon, having decided to return to the mainland with us, came aboard at three o'clock in the afternoon with their dogs and such of their household goods as they most prized; and by four we were shaping our course for Panama. There must be a subtle attraction in this solitary home, for, as the lofty peak of Mount Iglesias became lost to view in the mists of sunset, the tears welled up into the eyes of the Governor's wife.

Before his death in 1935, Gissler had insisted, "The treasure is on the island, but it will take money and a great deal of effort to unearth it. The work, once started, must be pushed strictly to an issue, otherwise some diplomatic land-sharks will reap the benefit of my work and investigations during the past twenty-two years. All this time, I have gone through many hardships and dangers, but I am willing to do so again and this will not keep me away. As soon as I obtain a guarantee that I can finish my work, I intend to start anew."[5]

5. *Dig for Pirate's Treasure*, Robert Nesmith, 1958.

Chapter 7

Shysters and Adventurers

*It seems we ne'er shall hear the last of Cocos
Island Treasure,
The tales of charlatans have led to follies out
of measure
They all have known just where it was, but
still the caves of Cocos
Refuse to yield their opulence, but keep it to
provoke us*

—*San Francisco Daily Morning
Call, March 19, 1872*

By the 1870s tales of fabulous treasures had spread from the Pacific Coast of Central and South America to California. Expedition after expedition, each claiming to have the authentic map to the treasure, came back empty handed. Yet they continued, and soon adventurers came to Cocos Island from all over the world. Most were inspired by the true story of Captain John Keating from Newfoundland, the only person known to have located the hiding place of the Lost Treasure of Lima. As the treasure hunting frenzy spread, those with means — and some knowledge of the Lima Treasure's history — sought the papers and maps allegedly handed down from Thompson to Keating, which they hoped would guide them to the loot.

The story of the Lost Treasure of Lima and its finding by Captain John Keating, is believed to have provided the general inspiration for Robert Louis Stevenson's classic novel *Treasure Island*.[1] Some writers say that Stevenson learned of the story while living in California in 1879 and 1880. San Francisco was the starting point of dozens of expeditions, and the prospectus circulated by each of the various expedition syndicates all mentioned Thompson, Bonito and Captain John Keating.

The Shysters

By the time Keating had returned to "Treasure Island" for a second withdrawal from the stolen treasure, tales of his first adventure were already known along the Pacific Coast of

---

1. The movie *Treasure Island*, based on Stevenson's novel, was produced by Walt Disney in 1950. In 1999 a remake was made, with Jack Palance as Captain Long John Silver.

South America. For the next one hundred years, Captain John Keating's story inspired more than four hundred expeditions in search of the Lost Treasure of Lima buried on Cocos Island.

Robert Nesmith, in the book *Dig for Pirates Treasure*, described treasure hunting fever inspired by the stories of the Lima Treasure and Captain Keating's success. He wrote:

> While enthusiastic adventurers were sailing under the auspices of old salts and ex-naval officers whose integrity was unquestioned, the greenhorns, excited by pirate lore and tales of gold, were clamoring to take off. Trawlers, ketches, yachts and schooners — anything able to carry a party and equipment — found a ready market. Cocos was overrun with diggers. The ever green public bought thousands of shares and waited for news that their syndicate had brought up the swag.

A treasure hunting syndicate operated out of San Francisco in the period from 1870 to the 1880s and financed a series of unsuccessful expeditions to Cocos Island. Its activities inspired a popular satirical poem published on March 19, 1872, in the San Francisco *Daily Morning Call* entitled, "The Legend of Cocos Island, Being the Revelations of an Ancient Mariner Concerning Sixty-five millions of Buried Treasure." The following is an excerpt from that poem:

> Again our ancient mariner, his curious yarn still spinning,
> Swears if he gets another show he's confident of winning;
> Explains the reason why the former expedition busted

Was that he feared the crew could not with so much
wealth be trusted.
He formed another company, and got some interested,
While others heard the wondrous tale, and doubted,
but invested.
"I'll titillate their hopes," thought he, "till they go up
like rockets:
If there's no treasure on the isle, there is in people's
pockets!"[2]

In 1901, Captain Fred Hackett and Captain A.B. Whidden
formed The Pacific Exploration and Development Co. Ltd. to
raise funds to finance another expedition in search of the Lost
Treasure of Lima. This treasure hunt was different than previous expeditions because a man named Justin Gilbert was
part of it, and he had a machine which he claimed could
locate gold and silver hidden beneath ground. The instrument
was supposed to do the work in twenty minutes which otherwise required months and possibly years to accomplish. The
Company explained that the instrument had located small
quantities of metal within a distance of two hundred yards,
and they anticipated it would easily locate a deposit the size of
the Lima Treasure for a distance of several miles.

The expedition located an eight inch ledge of ore 136 feet
below the ground. However, by the end of the search, and like
so many before it, this expedition ended in failure.[3]

In 1931, one such group of promoters, the Cocos Island
Treasure Company, aggressively pursued public investment in
a treasure hunting expedition to Cocos Island. They set up a
limited company in which they sold shares, offering investors
in return a share of the fabulous treasure that lay waiting to
be found on Cocos Island — also often referred to in pro-

2. *Dig for Pirates Treasure*, Robert Nesmith, 1958.
3. *Doubloons - The Story of Buried Treasure*, Charles H. Driscoll, 1931.

motional material as Treasure Island. The Cocos Island Treasure Ltd. was founded, and a persuasive prospectus was prepared and distributed. This prospectus outlined an interesting story in which little attention was paid to truth, and embellishments, exaggerations and false information were used to make a strong sales pitch.

The prospectus pamphlet gave a romantic and intriguing account of the treasures hidden on the pirates' paradise called Cocos Island. The first great treasure dealt with in the pamphlet was that of the seventeenth century pirate Captain Edward Davis. It described him as, "... a strong leader who never exhibited cruelty, inhumanity or brutality and who was implicitly trusted by all those who were under him." The pamphlet reported:

> Davis took gold and silver from Spanish galleons and buried it on Cocos Island. He built up a pirate organization of one thousand members and when this group became too hard to manage, Davis broke away and headed direct to Cocos Island where he added another several hundred pieces of eight to the cache already there. Soon afterwards, Davis pirated gold and jewels worth millions from the city of Guayquil.

Months before this he had added seven hundred thousand pieces of eight to his fortune on the Island.[4]

During one of Captain Davis' stays on Cocos Island a rather humorous incident occurred which was recorded in the diary of Doctor Lionel Wafer, who served under Davis and for whom Wafer Bay in Cocos Island is named. He told of the effect that excessive drinking of coconut milk had on the pirate crew. To entertain themselves the men cut down dozens of coconut trees, and extracted over twenty gallons of coconut milk. Dr. Wafer wrote:

---

4. *The Great Treasure Hunt*, Rupert Furneaux, 1931.

They sat down and drank health to the King and
Queen, and drank an excessive quantity of the milk.
Yet it did not end in drunkenness. This coconut liquor
so chilled and benumbed their nerves, that they could
neither go nor stand.

Nor could they return on board without the help
of those who had not been partakers of the frolic. It
took five days for these men to recover from the
effects of the coconut milk.

Throughout the five days the pirates were in a coma state,
and the defense of the pirates' position on Cocos Island was
weakened.[5]

The Davis Treasure may be added to the enormous fortune that remains hidden beneath the soil on Cocos Island. In
1930, the author A. Hyatt Verril wrote:

Nowhere in the history of Davis can be found any
statement to indicate that Davis ever removed his
treasures from Cocos Island — but then again neither
can we find any statement to the contrary. When
Davis retired from pirating he engaged in legitimate
business in the Orient from where he was subpoenaed
to appear as a witness in the trial against the pirate
Captain William Kidd.

The second treasure trove on Cocos Island mentioned in
the pamphlet was that of the infamous Benito 'Bloody Sword'
Bonito. The treasure buried by Bonito was estimated at 350
tons of gold boullion from lower California, Mexico and
Peru, which they valued at sixty million dollars.[6] The prospectus also claimed that Bonito was really a British officer named
Captain Bennett Graham.

---

5. *The Book of Buried Treasure*, Ralph D. Paine, 1922.
6. *The Romance of Buried Treasure*, T.C. Bridges, 1922.

The third treasure revealed was the famous Lost Treasure of Lima stolen by Captain Thompson in the brig *Mary Dear*. This treasure, the pamphlet claimed, included, "...all the gold and silver vessels and golden images from the Great Cathedral of Lima, valued at thirty million dollars." It reported that Thompson led a pirate's life for some years until his ship was captured. Thompson and one of the crew escaped, the rest were hanged. The prospectus read:

> The story of the treasures which lie hidden on this romantic and beautiful island is one which is colourful in the extreme and covers a period of nearly three centuries. It brings together notorious pirate chieftains, boisterous buccaneers, stately galleons, Spanish grandees and cavaliers, heroes and patriots, common thieves, mutineers, murderers, priests, and soldiers of fortune. Its ramifications extend from the South Seas to the Spanish Main, from mid-Pacific to the South Atlantic, from Madagascar to New England. Through it all one hears in imagination the refrain:
>
> *Fifteen men on the dead man's chest*
> *Yo-ho-ho, and a bottle of rum!"*[7]

The prospectus blended fact with fiction and spawned much of the conflicting and erroneous stories connected with Cocos Island since that time. It was used by many researchers and adventurers and has contributed ever since to muddy the waters regarding the Lost Treasure of Lima. When needed, promoters produced fraudulent eyewitness accounts to support their claims.

Perhaps the most impressive of the syndicates was the Spanish Main Exploration Company Limited, 1934. This firm was founded by Captain Charles Augustus Arthur, an aide-de-camp to Sir Hari Singh, the Maharajah of Kashmir. Arthur

7. *Dig for Pirates Treasure*, Robert Nesmith, 1958.

had served time in prison for participating in the blackmail of Sir Hari. This syndicate captured international attention and its leaders took part in a dramatic adventure that required a diplomatic effort from London to solve. Among those involved in the syndicate was Commander F.A. Worsley, who had been on two British Antarctic expeditions in 1921 and 1925 and Commander Joseph Russell Stenhouse, who had been Captain on Shackleton's Antarctic expedition in 1914-1916. The prospectus issued by this group was professionally printed and illustrated, featuring engravings of priceless Inca gold relics. Like all the others, this prospectus mixed fact and fiction and described the treasure as:

> Gold bars and specie worth ELEVEN MILLION DOLLARS from rifling churches in Peru; TWELVE MILLION DOLLARS buried by Thompson; buried by the notorious Bonito of the Bloody Sword — THREE HUNDRED AND FIFTY TONS of gold; by Davis the buccaneer THREE HUNDRED THOUSAND POUNDS WEIGHT IN SILVER DOLLARS, SEVEN HUNDRED AND THIRTY-THREE BARS OF GOLD, also SEVEN KEGS OF GOLD COIN. All on Cocos Island!

This syndicate did not rely on ancient maps and pages of instructions and directions to the Treasure Troves. Instead they offered:

> Under expert supervision, by proved electrical and electromagnetic methods, all areas likely to conceal treasure will be thoroughly and systematically explored with apparatus of not less than nine alternative methods, seven of which are selected whereby no conductive metals may escape detection.

This expedition received international attention when it consulted a clairvoyant, Gene Dennis, who forecast that the expedition was destined for success. The 700-ton steamship, the *Queen of Scots*, was donated for use by the syndicate by one of the investors in the venture. It set out for Cocos Island in early August 1934. The treasure hunters sent back progress reports on the venture. One read:

> Continuous rains — surf — shark-infested water — party safely ashore — impenetrable bush every-where — prospecting commenced — all optimistic. September 26, 1934.

The adventure took a dramatic turn in October when news reports received in London from San Jose disclosed that the treasure hunt had been forbidden, and the Costa Rican government had sent fifty police to arrest the group and take possession of the *Queen of Scots*. Diplomatic efforts succeeded in having the boat and crew-members released and they returned empty handed to England.

The Syndicate regrouped, and after obtaining approval from Costa Rico, returned to Cocos Island in an unsuccessful attempt to locate the treasure.[8]

Another group, the Treasure Island Expedition Syndicate, organized in London, England, defrauded the public of tens of thousands of dollars. This syndicate told a shorter story than the Cocos Island Treasure Ltd. But told it in larger print. It read:

BURIED BY BONITO IN 1818 & LATER, GOLD BARS AND SPECIE WORTH ELEVEN MIL-LION DOLLARS; BURIED BY THOMPSON, TWELVE MILLION DOLLARS; BURIED BY DAVIS, THREE HUNDRED THOUSAND

8. *The Great Treasure Hunt*, Rupert Furneaux, 1951.

POUNDS WEIGHT IN SILVER DOLLARS,
SEVEN HUNDRED AND THIRTY-THREE
BARS OF GOLD, ALSO SEVEN KEGS OF
GOLD COIN.

The pamphlet added that Bonito had buried an additional three hundred and fifty tons, consisting of bullion from
Lower California, Mexico and Peru.

Author Robert Nesmith believed that the source of the treasure clues and maps that adventurers sought before setting out
to seek treasure on Cocos Island was Captain Thompson. He
stated:

> To keep the Cocos treasure hunting activity alive
> for over a hundred years, very naturally there had to
> be documents or eyewitness tales to back up these
> statements. The principal source of information was
> the Captain Thompson documents. These were hand-
> ed down from Thompson to Keating. Keating was
> said to have passed them on to others.

Keating added his own written statement and letters to
those he received from Thompson. These became known as
the Thompson-Keating papers. Some years later, Keating is
alleged to have passed on this information to Captain Nick
Fitzgerald.

Whoever put together the Thompson-Keating papers —
which were circulated by treasure-hunting promoters — had
included some of the known portions of the treasure tale, and
embellished and added to the documents. However, there are
glaring inaccuracies in the letters which destroy their credibil-
ity. For example, the letter allegedly written by Thompson
refers to the Lima Treasure being stolen in 1835 during Simon
Bolivar's march on Lima.[9] Records show that the treasure was

9. *Doubloons,* Charles H. Driscoll, 1931.

actually stolen on August 19, 1821, and Simon Bolivar had died in December 1830. In the alleged letter from Captain John Keating, it is stated that the expedition was financed by merchants from St. John's, Newfoundland. In fact, it was financed by the Liverpool, England firm of Smith & Irwin, who owned the *Edgecombe* and sent along Captain Gault to protect their interests.

Keating, however, did find the treasure on two occasions. The only person to whom he is believed to have passed on a true version of the story given to him by Captain Thompson was Captain Nicholas Fitzgerald. After Fitzgerald shared that document with others and details became public, it too was embellished and changed by subsequent writers and promoters so that on its own merits today, it is no longer a dependable source of information. The original Thompson-Keating-Fitzgerald papers disappeared with the death of Captain Fitzgerald in 1906.

Adventurers

In 1892, a man named von Bremer spent thousands of dollars in making excavations on Cocos Island and drove some tunnels for upwards of a hundred yards underground, but there was no trace of any treasure. However, while researching Cocos Island, von Bremer had discovered a clue which convinced him he would find the treasure. He had acquired an alleged set of the Thompson-Keating papers that instructed him to seek a spot, "...from which the bearings of the points or lugs of Wafer Bay formed an angle of thirty-five degrees with one another." He followed the instructions but his efforts were fruitless.[10]

In 1902, a British Columbian brigantine, the *Blakeley,* carried a confident crew of treasure hunters to the lonely Pacific Island. They were under the command of the same Captain

10. *The Book of Buried Treasure,* Ralph D. Paine, 1922.

Hackett who had earlier accompanied Mrs. Brennan on the *Aurora* in 1894. The *Blakeley* expedition, like that of the *Aurora*, was a failure.[11]

In 1902 it seemed that after almost a half century of unsuccessful expeditions to Cocos Island, the Lost Treasure of Lima was about to be found. Captain James Brown convinced some wealthy businessmen in San Francisco that he was the only living person who knew exactly where the Lima Treasure was buried, and it was not on Cocos Island.

Captain Brown, then seventy-two years old, told a remarkable story of how he had teamed up with the son of Captain Thompson and successfully located the treasure on Cocos Island. He claimed they removed the entire treasure and took it to another isolated South Pacific island where they buried it. Brown said he later killed his partner in self defence, which left him the only living person who knew the location of the treasure site.

His story convinced the businessmen. They formed a company, invested money and purchased the schooner *Herman*. On June 2, 1902, they set sail from San Francisco for the Pacific. However, when the expedition experienced trouble finding the island, Brown offered a variety of excuses and sometimes lost his temper. It quickly became apparent that Captain Brown had no knowledge of the real hiding place of the Lima Treasure.

During his lifetime Brown had collected enough of the Cocos Island treasure story to bluff his backers and to be treated like royalty while he sailed the Pacific at their expense.

Another expedition which was mentioned by Montmorency was within feet of the treasure. When the leader of that effort described to Keating where he had dug, the old Captain jumped to his feet excitedly and exclaimed: "By God, you were within ten feet of the treasure!" Few other details of this event were recorded.[12]

11. *The Romance of Buried Treasure,* T.C. Bridges, 1931.
12. *Doubloons,* Charles H. Driscoll, 1931.

In 1904, the same year Herve de Montmorency's book on his first adventures to Cocos Island was released, the adventurer returned on a second expedition with Harold Gray on the *Rosmarine*. The majority of expeditions to the island sought the treasure based on questionable accounts of Keating's information given to Fitzgerald. The treasure hunters gained Gissler's confidence and Gissler joined in the search for the rock rising like a cliff which had been described in a Keating letter. The three men followed the stream referred to in the letter but were unable to find any cave. Through years searching the island and gathering information from the treasure seekers who came, Gissler had developed his own theory regarding the treasure. He reasoned that the *Relampago* had anchored between Chatham and Wafer Bays and Captain Bonito and his band of pirates had hoisted the treasure on to a plateau, three acres in extent, and seventy feet above the beach. The trio arrived at a site which they felt could be a hidden cave and after clearing the vegetation from the plateau they dug a trench to the depth of seven feet across the level ground. This effort failed to find any treasure.[13]

Around 1904-1905 a wealthy British Lord, who was believed to possess more wealth than the Lima Treasure was worth, actually purchased a liner, the *Harlech Castle*, to take his rich friends for an adventure to "Treasure Island", and to escape the boredom of club life in London. The visit to the island turned out to be anything but a vacation and treasure hunting game. Two rival expeditions arrived at Cocos island the same time and bloodshed was narrowly avoided. Expectations among the passengers of the *Harlech Castle* were high and they believed they could easily find the treasure trove in a few hours. When this failed, and they discovered that Cocos Island with its swarms of red ants, snakes, insects, and wild boars was not as pleasant a holiday resort as the French Riviera, they returned to England.

13. *The Book of Buried Treasure*, Ralph D. Paine, 1922.

One of the competing expeditions was led by Captain John Voss, who later became world famous for a canoe voyage around the world. Voss had information that the Lima Treasure was valued at thirty-five million dollars and weighed fifty tons. Gissler told Voss that even if he found the treasure the weight of the gold would sink his little ship. Voss's cutter, the *Xora*, weighed ten tons and came close to being shipwrecked when it became grounded on a reef in Wafer Bay. Although most of the provisions and gear were lost, the *Xora* made it to safety and returned to England empty handed.[14]

Another expedition that took place in 1904 sparked a mystery that was not solved until thirty years later. This episode, in the continuing story of the hunt for the Lost Treasure of Lima, began at Southampton, England during October 1904, when Earl Fitzwilliam organized one of the largest expeditions to seek treasure on Cocos Island. The adventure was shrouded in mystery from the start.

Fitzwilliam told the press that his party of fifty workers were going on a scientific expedition to South America to search for rare orchids and minerals. However, after visiting several South American ports, the Fitzwilliam yacht arrived at Puntarenas, Costa Rica where the Earl sparked an international incident. When the Costa Rican authorities refused to issue him a permit to dig for treasure on Cocos Island, he threatened that he could easily capture and take possession of Cocos Island if necessary. While the Costa Ricans protested to the British Government, Fitzwilliam ignored their authority and sailed on to the island where he anchored at Chatham Bay around mid-December.

At daybreak on New Year's Day, 1905, Gissler arrived at Chatham Bay and was appalled at what he discovered. There was evidence of a major change in the geography of the area, and the Fitzwilliam yacht had departed, leaving Chatham Bay deserted. Gissler later reported that dynamite had been used

14. *The Pacific,* Thomas Crowell, 1930

and caused a major landslide on a hill east of the waterfall. He said that if any treasure was in that area, it was now buried under tons of rock and dirt.

For the next thirty years, what had happened on Cocos Island on New Year's Eve, 1904 remained a mystery. Then, in 1934, an article appeared in *Blackwood's Magazine* written by David Smith, who had been a member of the Fitzwilliam expedition. In the article, Smith recalled the full story of the Fitzwilliam expedition.

According to Smith, Fitzwilliam became impatient after several days of digging failed to turn up any evidence of a treasure. He concluded that the geography of the area had changed so drastically over the previous fifty years that maps were no longer of any value. The expedition leader then decided if there was any treasure in the general area indicated on the map, the use of dynamite would expose it. Smith wrote:

We placed the powder beneath a large rock near the waterfall. The resulting explosion was not so great as we expected. We rushed to the cliff. I was easily the winner, and had just reached the goal, when crash! The earth beneath me shook, the whole face of the rock seemed to rise up, twist, and lean over. Stones weighing tons and pounds (sic) hurtled past and over me. Someone had miscalculated in setting the fuses. I was up to my waist in rubble. I had not a bruise or scratch on my body, but of a dozen men on the hillside, I was standing alone. Fitzwilliam was the first to rise, staggering about blinded by blood from a ghastly wound running across his scalp. He tried to take command of the situation, refusing all offers of attention. We had to fill him with brandy to keep him quiet and enable us to dress his wound.

Those who were uninjured evacuated the injured to the yacht and disbanded their camp site. Fortunately, the expedition included a doctor who tended the injured until the vessel arrived at Panama where they were taken to a hospital.

The incident caused some diplomatic trouble between England and Costa Rica and when Fitzwilliam arrived back in London, he was summoned to Buckingham Palace where he was to be given 'a heavy wigging' from the King. However, King Edward VII was a true gentleman and had the common touch. When he rose from his chair, he told Smith, 'You know perfectly well you ought not to have done it, but by God, I wish I had been with you."[15]

In 1925, then world famous Sir Malcolm Campbell and Lee Guinness went to Cocos Island with high hopes of finding the treasure.[16] They had collected the Thompson-Keating-Fitzgerald records along with some charts and related documents. Once on the island, Campbell quickly concluded that the treasure was hidden at Chatham Bay. Hopes ran high among the treasure hunters when they found the entrance to a cave. It was covered in, as if by some sort of landfall, and had to be dug out. Bridges noted:

> After removing a number of large boulders they came to a wall of cut stones, and levered these out, one by one. But behind were stones so much larger that it was impossible to shift them. Almost too weary to walk, they dragged themselves back to their camp.

Next day the digging resumed, and although no treasure was found, Campbell concluded that the wall was part of an ancient Inca Sun Temple, which proved that Cocos Island, like many uninhabited islands in the Pacific, at one time had been the home of some prosperous people. A change in the weather forced the Campbell expedition to leave the island. Although he gave up the hunt, he left the island convinced that the treasure cave existed. He suggested that the reason

15. *Dig for Pirates' Treasure*, Robert Nesmith, 1958.
16. *The Romance of Buried Treasure*, T. C. Bridges, 1931.

for the failure of the Spaniards to find the *Mary Dear*'s treasure was that no digging operation had been needed to hide the loot. After burying the treasure, Campbell said, the pirates caused a landslide to hide the site.

In 1931, Campbell published a book entitled *My Greatest Adventure,* in which he put forward the theory that Keating had murdered Boag by shutting him up in the treasure cave and leaving him to starve to death. While researching this story I found an account of the successful Keating-Boag expedition in 1841, which was written by Boag's grandson. That story is told in a previous chapter and disproves the Campbell theory which was picked up by many subsequent writers on the subject and was the source of many inaccurate accounts. According to the Boag family, Captain Boag drowned under mysterious circumstances at Panama. Only his arm was recovered from the waters and that was buried in the cemetery at Panama City.

The terrain on Cocos Island had changed since 1821 when Thompson hid the treasure. Campbell found evidence of this when he set fire to an area of brush to clear some of the jungle growth obstructing their search. The wind changed and Campbell and party retreated to the beach until the fire exhausted itself. Campbell then discovered a zig-zag track leading up the hillside. He discovered a dried up bed of a stream and found that its course had been diverted by a great landslide. Other landmarks essential to finding the treasure had also disappeared.[17]

A man named P.A. Bergman, who was a passenger on the vessel *Westward* which, in 1929, had been chartered by a Holywood movie company, related a fascinating tale of how he had stumbled on a fabulous treasure while marooned on Cocos Island, and over subsequent years had been pursued by New York gangsters.[18]

17. *The Romance of Treasure,* T.C. Bridges, 1951.
18. *Dig For Pirates Gold,* 1958.

When the *Westward* encountered a tropical storm off the coast of Nicaragua, Bergman and Captain H. Peterson escaped in a lifeboat and drifted for several days before sighting an island which turned out to be Cocos Island. The two found refuge in an abandoned house left by Gissler. A week or more passed without any sight of a rescue ship. While wandering the Island, Bergman stepped on a spot that gave way under his weight, and when he removed his foot, he could clearly see an opening in the ground.

He removed some of the surrounding earth and discovered the entrance to a cave. Bergman managed to get into the cave where he found himself surrounded by a fabulous treasure of glittering gold, silver and gems. He described the measurements of the cave as about forty yards by fifteen yards. He also claimed that he found parchments bearing the name of Benito Bonito, which he removed and later stored in a safe deposit box at San Francisco.[19]

Bergman listed the contents of the cave which he, in 1934, passed on to a syndicate which used the document in promoting shares in its venture. It reads as follows:

> When arriving in the cave you will first notice on your left the form of a person (skeleton). Further on the left are sacks with gold nuggets, and more sacks further inside on the same left. You will have to walk on silver coins, and other metals found in abundance. On the right from the entrance are seven little barrels containing gold coins, and in the middle are eight boxes or trunks, and many different pieces of ornament from churches placed together with statuettes. Two of the boxes have been opened by me, and jewels have been removed. Notice an old shirt was used to make a sack from, but was later left in the cave, and gold nuggets of all sizes were taken from the sacks

19. In 1931, *Treasure Hunt* magazine reported that Bergman had found a two-foot-high gold Madonna in the Bay of Hope, which he sold in New York for $11,000.

and spread on the ground so two of the bags could be used to fill them with jewels.

Bergman brought Peterson who, although ill, assisted in removing and hiding on the island two sacks of gold, after which they concealed the entrance to the cave. When an abandoned lifeboat washed up on the shore of Wafer Bay, the two used it to leave the island. They were rescued by a German boat under command of Captain Heindritch. The Captain offered to help them sell the items taken from the treasure cave and he brought them to New York where they were introduced to an underworld firm of dealers. They were paid $56,000 for the loot, an amount which was lower than the treasure's true value. After the deal, and the splitting up of the money, the three men went their separate ways. Peterson died at Portland, Oregon in 1932, and Bergman moved to Europe.

In 1934, Bergman, running out of money, decided to seek help in going back for more treasure. He found support from a Chicago lawyer named Colonel Hunter who, after satisfying himself that Bergman was telling the truth, made his own yacht, the *Nautilis,* available for the expedition.

On the trip to the island, the ship's cook warned Bergman that his life was in danger. Bergman led the others in circles around Wafer Bay, pretending he couldn't find the treasure cave. Finally Hunter gave up, and during a stopover at Panama, Bergman was beaten up and required hospitalization. When he was released, Hunter took him back on board and later dropped him off at Trinidad.

From there Bergman teamed up with a man he had met while in Panama. George Lane was a British ex-naval officer who had worked for the Colombian government in training men for their new gunboats. Bergman claimed he had been shadowed by agents of an underworld firm and Hunter, who believed that he would lead them back to the treasure. Lane took on the job as Bergman's bodyguard.

Bergman later turned up on Cocos Island as part of the *Queen of Scots* expedition. He showed them the place where he had hid the two bags of loot, but was unable to find the cave. The Bergman information was used in the prospectus of the syndicate that sponsored the *Queen of Scots* expedition, and may not be credible.

At the time of the Bergman expeditions there was almost universal belief that Keating had killed Boag and sealed him inside the treasure cave. This was totally inaccurate and suggests the story may have been contrived to inspire investors' confidence in one of the many syndicates set up to seek the lost treasure. Boag family accounts of the death of Captain William Boag included in this book contradict the killed-in-the-cave theory.

Another remarkable story putting forward new clues to the hiding place of the Lima Treasure emerged in 1960 in the book *The Lost Treasure of Cocos Island*, by Ralph Hancock and Julian A. Weston. This story challenges other stories that claim the pirate of the Lima Treasure of 1821 was Captain Thompson.[20]

A claim emerged in the early twentieth century that the true leader of the pirates of the Lima Treasure was a man named James Alexander Forbes, according to Hancock and Weston. Forbes, they said, was a medical doctor who shipped as mate on the *Mary Dear* on her maiden voyage from Bristol to South America (sic). Forbes led the crew in mutiny against Captain Marion Thompson, took command of the ship and participated in the murder of the guards and priests. Thompson is said to have been a reluctant participant in the subsequent piracy and burial at Cocos Island of the Lima Treasure. Forbes chose the hiding site which was described as:

> A place not too obvious from where it could be easily recovered. Discovering that beneath the beach

20. *The Great Treasure Hunt*, Rupert Furneaux, 1968.

ran a shelf of rock visible only at low tide, and strong enough to carry the weight of the gold, he instructed his men to dig a deep hole below the high water mark, into which the eleven (sic) boatloads of treasure were tipped, an operation that took between tides several days.

After the hole had been filled in, a big square boulder weighing several tons was dragged across the beach and maneuvered on top. Finally Forbes cut the design of an anchor on the boulder and took accurate bearings by which to rediscover the spot. To make doubly sure, Forbes diverted the course of the stream that flowed into the bay, so that it made its exit some distance from his cache.

According to this version, Forbes escaped to Puentarenas and was believed to have died. However, he turned up later in California, a colony of Spain at the time. Some years later, he returned to Cocos Island and recovered enough of the treasure to make him a wealthy man, and started several businesses. He passed the secret of the treasure along with a map and instructions on to his son. In 1939, James III, Forbes' grandson, made an unsuccessful attempt to recover the treasure.

The weakness in this version and others that claimed to have maps from a person, or persons involved in hiding the treasure, is the only one that located the treasure was Keating, who got his information from Thompson. Keating, not once but twice, succeeded in finding the treasure. The sons of James Forbes III used the alleged inherited treasure map to promote many expeditions to Cocos Island. This version has many similarities to the Cabral version told in an earlier chapter in this book.

The claim that Dr. Forbes signed on with the *Mary Dear* at Bristol could not have been based on fact. It was shown earlier in this book that the *Mary Dear* was the name given to a vessel captured by pirates and as such would not have been at Bristol under that name.

In 1948, Harry and Betty O'Hanlon visited Newfoundland to research the Keating-Fitzgerald connection to the Lost Treasure of Lima. They left Newfoundland confident enough to make their own treasure-hunting expedition that year to Cocos Island. The two adventurers were joined by Tim Eagan of California, a veteran of two previous expeditions in search of the Lima Treasure, one in 1939 and the second in 1946. Both adventures had ended in failure. On his second expedition, on a vessel named the *Tradewinds*, he suffered an injury and had to cut short his search. He left Cocos Island with the intention of returning. Harry and Betty O'Hanlon offered him that opportunity. Eagan's involvement inspired optimism in the O'Hanlon's who were further encouraged by having a metal detector with them.

Eagan knew well the geography of the Island and also had knowledge of a recent interesting discovery made on Cocos Island. Captain Tim Cullen, a San Diego fisherman, had told Eagan of a discovery made by a friend from San Francisco, named Milton Canham, and his brother. While the two were bathing in a stream on the Island they walked beneath a waterfall running into the stream. Milton noticed something bright in the water, and stopped to retrieve it. The item turned out to be a bar of solid gold. Eagan said the item was sold in San Francisco for $35,000. He told the O'Hanlon's it was this story that had sparked his own expeditions in search of the treasure.[21]

The trio had chartered a boat from Puentarenas to bring them to Cocos Island and now the boat returned on schedule to get them. This forced an end to the expedition without finding the Lost Treasure of Lima. The metal detector turned out to be a total failure. Betty O'Hanlon explained:

---

21. *True Tales of Pirates and Their Treasures,* Edward R. Snow, 1953.

The island being of volcanic origin, there is much magnetite in the rocks, and this renders a metal detector almost useless.

Tim Eagan, however, had some luck. He found several gold doubloons in a stream near Chatham Bay, perhaps the same stream where Canham found his gold bar and Montmorency his silver cross. Betty O'Hanlon wrote a feature article on the Lima Treasure and the Keating connection in the June 1964 edition of the *Atlantic Advocate*. The article gave little in the way of new information on the story and contained some of the popular beliefs about the Lima story at the time. She revealed very little in the article about her own adventure to Cocos Island in 1948.

One of the weirdest expeditions to search for the treasure was that of a British syndicate which used a medium to contact the spirit of the pirate Benito 'Bloody Sword' Bonito, who buried in excess of twelve million dollars on Cocos Island. The psychic claimed she saw a vision of Bonito, a tormented soul, walking the beach at Cocos Island and imploring that someone come and find the treasure. She conversed with him and he gave her directions to the treasure trove and said his soul could not rest until the treasure was found and put to a worthy use. The syndicate used the information in their advertisements. The expedition ended in failure and the only treasure from the trip was that made by the promoters of the expedition.[22]

Others attracted to Cocos Island by the Lost Treasure of Lima included: President Franklyn D. Roosevelt,[23] who visited Cocos Island in 1935, 1937 and 1940; movie star Errol Flynn; and Victor Hervey, a descendent of Lord Cochrane whom he claimed left clues to the treasure in his papers.

22. *Doubloons*, Charles H. Hutchings, 1931.
23. *1001 Lost, Buried, or Sunken Treasures*, F.L Coffman, 1957.

Prior to going to Cocos Island, the two adventurers, Harry and Betty O'Hanlon, carried out research in Newfoundland and left firmly convinced the Keating map was still in existence in this province. That could very well be. The map and letters of Keating and Fitzgerald may today be gathering dust in an attic or basement, or lost among the pages of an old family bible somewhere in Newfoundland. Meanwhile, the secret of the Lost Treasure of Lima appears to have died with Captain John Keating in 1882, and the fortune, estimated in today's value at one hundred to three hundred million dollars, lies buried forever beneath the soil on Cocos Island, which today is a world heritage site.

Chapter 8

The True Pirate and Treasure

There were two separate treasures stolen from Lima and buried on Cocos Island. There were two Captain Thompsons sailing in Peru during 1821 when the Mary Dear pirated one of the Lima Treasures. To add even more confusion to the story, part of the treasure stolen from the Peruvian churches was buried on the island of Trinidad off the coast of Brazil. Cocos Island also had buried treasure other than the Lima Treasures.

After the death of Captain Thompson in St. John's in 1840, and Captain John Keating's two successful recoveries from the cave concealing the Lost Treasure of Lima, an era of treasure hunting expeditions followed. The adventurers began seeking and collecting information about the treasure, and about Keating and Thompson, with expectations that the information would lead them to its secret hiding place on Cocos Island. Each expedition added new information to the treasure's history, and in time the multiple clues, directions, and maps began spawning several versions of the Treasure story.

While researching this book and piecing together a wealth of new information, I was able to determine that not only were there two separate Lima Treasures, but two separate Captain Thompsons. The first was Captain William Thompson, a Scottish-born man identified by pirate historians as the pirate of the Lima Treasure. The second was the true pirate, also named Thompson, and whom I identified as Captain Marion Thompson.

Many who have told the Lost Treasure of Lima story did so unaware that there were actually two Lima treasures buried on Cocos Island, and both were added to the existing loot hidden there. The first of the Lima Treasures was buried sometime during 1819 and 1820 by the notorious pirate of the Caribbean, Benito 'Bloody Sword' Bonito. *The World Atlas of Treasure* identifies Bonito as a former British naval officer named Captain Graham Bennett. A different claim is made in *On The Track of Treasure*, which claims he was a broken down Spanish or Portugese gentleman of good family, and was born at Pomaron, a town which stands on a river of the same name separating Portugal from Spain. The same book claims Bonito spoke several languages, including French and English. The second Lima Treasure buried on the Island was pirated on August 19, 1821, by Captain Thompson of the *Mary Dear*.

The events leading up to Bonito's piracy from churches at Lima began in 1814. Benito Bonito was a crewmember of a privateer ship that captured two vessels, the *Rosario* and the *Devonshire*. The *Devonshire* later played a major role in the story of the Lost Treasure of Lima. *The Rosario*, at 235 tons, was the larger of the two captured vessels. At the time of capture it was under the command of Captain J. Gaspar, and was operating between Portugal and Brazil, and also Liverpool to Lisbon.

The *Devonshire*, seventy-four tons, was under command of Captain J. Duniam and operated between Liverpool, England, St. John's, Newfoundland, and the West Indies. The privateers renamed the *Devonshire*, likely calling it the *Mary Dear*, and turned it into a privateer ship. This opinion is drawn from reports in the Lloyd's of London Shipping Records from 1814 to 1820, and references by author F. L. Coffman to the Lima Treasure as the *Devonshire Treasure*.

During August 1818 Bonito led a mutiny, which ended in the murder of his Captain. Lloyd's of London Records for 1818, without naming Bonito, describes a mutiny on the *Pelican* and the murder of its Captain. The leader of that mutiny then raised the Jolly Roger and led his pirates in capturing a slave ship at Cuba. This story is parallel in all details to the story of Bonito's mutiny and murder of his privateer captain and subsequent capture of a slave ship. The conclusion to be drawn from this is Bonito had been Captain of the *Pelican*.

The following month on September 21, 1818, Bonito attacked and plundered the *Columbia,* which was on a voyage from Cuba to Bristol. According to Lloyd's of London registers:

The *Columbia* was boarded by the pirates and plundered of all her cargo, besides 1,722 dollars in specie. Mr. W. Williams, a passenger, was robbed at the same time of 700 dollars. The crew of the *Pelican* treated Captain Gilbert with the greatest cruelty and even stripped him of his wearing apparel. They stated to Captain Gilbert that they had murdered their former commander a few days previous and had a very good mind to put him to death. Next day, September 22, the same pirates plundered the schooner *Alonzo Smith* of New York, and beat its captain most cruelly.

Courtesy Carter-Fitzgerald Black & White Photography

Jack Fitzgerald researching at the Maritime History Archives. The Lloyd's of London records located at the MHA were essential in unraveling the adventures of Captain Keating, Captain Thompson, the *Mary Dear*, and the *Edgecombe*.

Before leaving the West Indies, Bonito transferred the *Rosario*'s treasure to his own ship and then scuttled the *Rosario*. Circumstances suggest that Bonito, while on the Pacific Coast, commanded the *Relampago* and placed Thompson in command of the *Devonshire*. He abandoned seventeen of his men at Valparaiso and sailed off to the West Indies in the *Relampago*.

Bonito's connection with Cocos Island began in 1818, after he moved his pirate operations from the Caribbean to the Pacific. Treasure he had stolen in the Caribbean was buried on the island of Trinidad, off the Brazilian coast. When the existence of that treasure was revealed in later years, it added to the confusion over the Cocos Island treasures. After rounding the Horn on his journey to the Pacific, Bonito succeeded in pirating a large treasure of gold from a Spanish galleon, followed by more gold and silver taken from smaller Spanish vessels. He came upon Cocos Island, which he believed was an ideal place to hide this loot. The island had several ancient man-made caves — believed to have been constructed by Incas — which could easily be sealed and hidden. It was an uninhabited, inhospitable island which did not encourage permanent settlement.

Bonito continued to pirate ships on the Pacific, but during 1819 and 1820, he had found an easy target for pirate raids in the Roman Catholic churches of Peru. After stealing a load of treasure from the churches in Lima, he faced a mutiny when he returned to Cocos Island. The problem developed when Bonito suggested they return to the West Indies to recover the loot they had buried there, and bring it back to Cocos Island to add to that treasure. The men, however, had other ideas. They argued that they had been pirates long enough and it was now time to share the booty. Bonito drew his sword, and by morning fifteen buccaneers were lying in a pool of blood on the beach of Chatham Bay.[1]

---

1. *On the Track of Treasure*, Herve de Montmorency, 1904.

Rather than risk losing everything, the pirate captain suggested the mutiny be settled by dividing the treasure among the captain, officers and crew. The agreement was one portion would go to the captain, a second for the officers, and the third for the crew. The divided treasure was hidden at three different sites on Cocos Island with a map being drawn for each. Bonito then set sail for the West Indies to recover his treasure there, and planned to return to bury it at Cocos Island.

Some of those under Bonito's command expressed a wish to stop over at Valparaiso, Chili, for some rest and relaxation. Bonito agreed, and seventeen men decided to avail of this opportunity. Bonito promised to wait for their return. The pirate captain would have had at least two ships in his possession at this time — the *Relampago* and the *Devonshire* (*Mary Dear*). Most of those who were involved in the mutiny on Cocos Island were among the group to go ashore at Valparaiso. Once they were out of sight, Bonito raised anchor and abandoned them to sail to the West Indies. The band of seventeen pirates were recognized and captured at Valparaiso, and all but two were executed.

The two men who were spared at Valparaiso were Thompson and Chapelle. They had successfully pleaded for their lives by claiming they had been captured and forced into piracy by Bonito, and they promised to help the English track down and capture Bonito and his band of pirates. Armed with information from Thompson and Chapelle, the British naval ship the *Espiegel* caught up with Bonito in the West Indies. Bonito was not prepared to be taken prisoner and led his men in a spirited battle. When it became apparent that neither a victory nor an escape was possible, Bonito drew his pistol and shot himself. The English found several golden candlesticks on Bonito's ship, which they believed were pirated from a Peruvian church.

The following reveals the separate treasures buried by Bonito. On his first landing at Cocos Island, Bonito is reported to have buried the following loot, valued at twelve million dollars.

700 gold bars, 2x4 inches, and plate (unprocessed silver).

150 tons of silver and plate.

273 gold swords, ornamented with precious stones.

Other jewelry and church ornaments.

These items were buried on a small piece of land located in the middle of a stream, believed to be Wafer Creek.

In addition, he buried several iron kettles of gold coins and a bulk of heavier loot in a cave in the hills. This treasure was hidden by a landslide deliberately caused under orders from the pirate captain. Bonito was known to favour causing landslides to conceal his buried treasures.[2]

Just as Thompson had survived to tell tales of hidden treasure on Cocos Island, there was a survivor or two from Bonito's pirate campaigns who lived to pass on maps and directions to the loot buried by Bonito. Confusing the matter even more is the fact that the Captain Thompson who stole the 1821 treasure had served with Bonito in 1820 when the first Lima Treasure was stolen and buried.

The Lima Treasure that inspired the tradition of the Lost Treasure of Lima story was the one stolen on August 29, 1821, by Captain Marion Thompson of the *Mary Dear*. There are several conflicting itemized listings of the Lima Treasure, stolen by Captain Thompson and buried on Cocos Island. The value was estimated between eleven and twelve million dollars. One estimate listed the following items:

Two life-sized figures in pure gold of the Virgin and child (750 pounds each).

273 jeweled swords.

An immense treasure in gems, especially emeralds and minted coins valued at twelve million dollars.[3]

2. *1001 Lost, Buried or Sunken Treasures*, F.L. Coffman, 1957.

3. *The Romance of Buried Treasure*, T.C. Bridges, 1931.

It is interesting to note the lists of contents of both treasures contain the item 273 jeweled swords. Similarities in both treasure stories further demonstrates the merging of the two stories that has taken place since Captain John Keating's second visit to the treasure in 1845.

According to author T. C. Bridges, Thompson had confided to Keating the existence of two treasures buried on Cocos Island. Bridges' version claimed that Thompson had told Captain Keating that he (Thompson) was present when Bonito buried 300,000 pounds of silver dollars and valuables which were stored in a sandstone cave in the side of a hill. This information was in reference to the loot buried on Cocos Island during Bonito's first visit there. Gunpowder was used by the pirates to cause a landslide that buried all traces of the treasure. Thompson also told Captain Keating that more treasure was buried in a second cave. That treasure consisted of 733 gold bricks, 4 x 3 x 2 inches. In a third burial site on a piece of land close by a stream, the pirates buried several kettles of gold coin. This treasure was the one pirated on the *Mary Dear*. After confiding these secrets to Keating, Thompson added, "All these I could find if I can reach the Island."

Montmorency estimated the treasure stolen by Thompson, which he valued at $11,000,000, would form a "...bulky mass weighing over sixteen tons and having the capacity of thirty-two or thirty-three cubic feet. The cave then must be a large one." The Lima treasure has been estimated at various amounts between $11,000,000 and $70,000,000. The discrepancies are due to the fact that not all the treasure taken to Callao ended up on the *Mary Dear*.

The World Atlas of Treasure, Derek Wilson, 1981, London, published a more specific inventory of the stolen Lima Treasure which contains some details on the hiding of the loot.

Quoting what is believed to be Thompson's inventory statement, Wilson writes:

We have buried at a depth of four feet in red
earth:

One chest: altar trimmings of cloth of gold, with
baldachins, monstrances, chalices, comprising 1,244
stones.

One chest: two gold reliquaries weighing 120
pounds, with 624 topazes, cornelians and emeralds,
twelve diamonds.

One Chest: three reliquaries of cast metal weighing 160 pounds, with 860 rubies and various stones,
nineteen diamonds.

One Chest: 4,000 doubloons of Spain marked 8,
5,000 crowns of Mexico, 124 swords, 64 dirks, 120
shoulder belts, twenty-eight rondaches (small shields).

One Chest: eight caskets of cedar wood and silver,
with 3,840 cut stones, rings, patens and 4,265 uncut
stones.

Twenty-eight feet to the north-east at a depth of
eight feet in the yellow sand — seven chests with
twenty-two candelabra in gold and silver, weighing
250 pounds, and 164 rubies.

Twelve arm spans west, at a depth of ten feet in
the red earth. The seven-foot Virgin of gold with the
child Jesus and her crown and pectoral of 780 pounds,
rolled in her gold chasuble on which are 1,684 jewels.
Three of these are four inch emeralds on the pectoral
and six are six-inch topazes on the crown. The seven
crosses are diamonds.

In addition to the confusion caused by two separate Lima
Treasures was the fact that there were — as mentioned earlier in this chapter — two Captain Thompsons in Peru in 1821.
A factor not known by Cocos Island treasure seekers since
that time is that the pirate Captain Thompson was the same
Thompson who was pressed into piracy by Benito Bonito
when he took the *Lightning*. This explains why Captain

Thompson of the *Mary Dear* had knowledge of Bonito's treasures on Cocos Island, as well as that of the Lima Treasure stolen in 1821. He shared his knowledge of both treasures with Captain John Keating. Historians and adventurers focused on the Scottish-born Captain William Thompson as the pirate of the Lima Treasure, and by following that trail, a large body of erroneous information became incorporated into the Lost Treasure of Lima story.

Captain Keating's successes in 1840 and 1845 inspired more than four hundred expeditions in search of the Lost Treasure of Lima. The many searches for the real map and directions to the treasure brought together the information that had emerged from several sources in the South Seas with the information revealed by Thompson in Newfoundland. Over time the two very different treasure stories blended into one. Lost among all of this was the truth, and the result was the failure by any of the treasure-hunting expeditions to find the Lima Treasure.

Some years passed after the *Mary Dear* had stolen the Lima Treasure and news of the piracy and murder committed by Captain Thompson had spread throughout the world. The story was told and retold, and was written about in newspapers on several continents. It became an accepted part of the Lima Treasure story that the Captain Thompson who pirated the Lima Treasure was the Scottish-born Captain William Thompson. This same Captain Thompson was well known throughout South American ports, and in particular, Callao, where he frequently visited to deliver and pick up cargoes. The real pirate had escaped public attention.

In researching material for this book and tracing Thompson's movements from 1820 to 1840 through Lloyd's of London Shipping Records, it soon became clear that Captain William Thompson was not a pirate. In fact, he had worked throughout his life as a trusted sea captain who had sailed the seven seas and was respected in many countries including Newfoundland. It was also becoming clear that there was a second Captain Thompson.

Edward R. Snow, author of *True Tales of Pirates and Their Gold*, 1953, and one of the almost two dozen authors of books on the subject of the Lost Treasure of Lima, claimed the whole story was a myth. He charged, and rightly so at the time, that nobody had sought to verify the existence of the *Mary Dear*, Captain Thompson, nor that a treasure was stolen from Lima during the Spanish American revolution. Indeed, the many books written about the Spanish American revolution do not mention any treasure being stolen from Lima, nor do they mention Captain Thompson and the *Mary Dear*.

After learning of this, I reviewed a majority of the books on the subject which had bibliographies, and determined that none had searched Lloyd's of London Records, nor archival records in Newfoundland, which had a close and essential connection with the story.

While it was possible to trace the pirate Captain Thompson through these records, and to verify the date and value of the treasure stolen from Lima, there was no record to show that a ship named the *Mary Dear* — or the several other names by which it was known, the *Mary Dier, Mary Read* — ever existed. This, however, should not be surprising. The *Mary Dear* was a pirate ship and would not have used its registered name. As I have mentioned elsewhere in this book, I believe the *Mary Dear* was the *Devonshire* which was pirated by Bonito and Thompson when they sailed together. However, there was some truth in Thompson's claims when first captured, that he was forced into piracy.

In 1814, an American firm, the Carterit Company, had a new ship built at Liverpool, England, and christened the *Lightning*. Initially the *Lightning* was to carry cargoes between England and Newfoundland. Thompson, at a youthful age, became a crewman on the *Lightning*, but historical records do not show whether he did so, either in England or in St. John's, Newfoundland. His close friend, a man named Chapelle, served in St. John's as an officer in the Royal Navy in 1813, and the following year was serving on the *Lightning*. Possibly the two men joined the crew of the *Lightning* at St. John's. The ship made many trips to St. John's between 1814 and 1817, until its owners found a more lucrative purpose for it.

It was the era of Africans being captured and sold as slaves in North and South America. The *Lightning's* owners learned of the demand and the good prices being offered for slaves in Portuguese Brazil. The native Indians of Brazil, unlike those in the Andes, were considered to be inept and unreliable workers. Portuguese landowners turned to the African slave markets for prospective labourers. On one occasion when the *Lightning* had dropped off its human cargo of slaves at Rio de Janeiro, and was on a stopover at Metanzas, Cuba, on a return voyage to Africa for more slaves, she was sighted by one of the last great pirates of the Caribbean and South Pacific — Captain Benito 'Bloody Sword' Bonito.

In July 1818, after taking control of the *Pelican* and turning to piracy, Bonito sought a bigger and faster ship. It was at this time that he crossed paths with the *Lightning* at Metanzas, Cuba. Under cover of darkness, the pirates entered Metanzas Harbour and took over the *Lightning*, after cutting it from its moorings. Once arriving at a safe distance from Cuba , Bonito transferred to the *Lightning,* where he lowered the British flag and replaced it with the Jolly Roger. He then renamed it the *Relampago* (Spanish for chain lightning). All except two of the British crew were forced to walk the plank. Two young men, Thompson and Chapelle, a Quebecer, begged for their lives and offered to join Benito's pirate band. Benito was in need of extra men to sail his prizes to secret ports, where he would plunder the cargoes and perhaps add a ship to his command.

At this point I began tracing the moves of the pirate Thompson, and the information gathered began to reveal that there were two Captain Thompsons. To untangle the story required searching several years of Lloyd's of London Records, most of them not indexed. At times it seemed like I was looking for a needle in a haystack.

In the records of 1817, I confirmed that while the pirate Thompson was serving on the *Lightning* in 1817, the Scottish Captain William Thompson was serving as captain of the *Alcyon*, sailing out of Brazil. While the pirate Captain Thompson was burying treasure on Cocos Island in August 1821, the Scottish Thompson was serving as Captain of the *Elizabeth* visiting ports in Demerara (Guyana today), Brazil and Cuba. Just two months after the captain and crew of the *Mary Dear* buried the Lima Treasure on Cocos Island, the Scottish Captain William Thompson was involved in a rescue operation near Cuba. On October 15, 1821, a ship named the *Cuba* ran into trouble off the coast of Cuba and remained adrift for forty-eight hours. Thompson came to its aid and rescued the entire crew.[4]

After 1821, the Scottish Thompson's career was not one a pirate would ever consider following. The treasure was stolen on August 19, 1821, and four months later the Scottish Captain Thompson was in the port of Callao where the crime took place. He remained there for a couple of months, then took the British ship *Rebecca* to Valparaiso, Chili, the headquarters for the Patriot Forces of San Martin and Lord Thomas Cochrane.

Lloyd's records show that over the next twenty years Thompson, unmolested by authorities, sailed in and out of South American ports, including Cocos Island. No man wanted for piracy would have been bold enough to sail throughout the world, visiting ports using his own name and credentials. The penalty for piracy was execution, and in England it included being drawn and quartered — partially hanged, then disemboweled and the hanging resumed. Yet his journeys over the next twenty years suggest that for some reason, he was on the trail of the Thompson who stole the Lima Treasure.

4. Lloyd's of London Shipping Movements, October 1821, Maritime History Archives, Memorial University of Newfoundland.

The two Thompsons may have been related and part of the famous seafaring Thompson family of Scotland. This would explain why the Captain William Thompson of the *Rebecca* appeared to be shadowing the pirate Thompson at Cocos Island; Metanzaz, Cuba; Liverpool, England and St. John's, Newfoundland. Perhaps the Scottish Thompson was trying to protect a younger brother.

The same week during May 1840, when the pirate Thompson arrived with Keating in St. John's, Captain William Thompson arrived there on the *Donegal*. Even more intriguing is that when Keating, Boag and Thompson went to Liverpool during November, 1840, to meet with Smith and Irwin, Captain William was also there taking command of a Newfoundland-owned ship, the *Dewsbury*. When the others returned to Newfoundland in late November or early December, 1840, Captain William Thompson left Sligo, Ireland to deliver the *Dewsbury* to its part owner — Thomas Gamber, of Carbonear, Newfoundland. Months after Captain John Keating returned from his second expedition to Cocos Island, having sailed there in a ship of which he was half owner with James Stewart, the Scottish Captain William Thompson turned up in Nova Scotia as captain of a ship owned by J & W Stewart. Although the Scottish William Thompson was not a pirate, the mystery of his relationship and apparent shadowing of the pirate Captain Thompson may never be solved.

As if two Captain Thompsons and two separate Lima Treasures were not confusing enough, a claim emerged that the Lima Treasure was buried on Trinidad Island and not Cocos Island. This theory was put forward in the mid-twentieth century. The confusion, no doubt, arose from the fact that some of the treasure stolen from Lima in 1821 ended up buried at Trinidad. I pointed out earlier that not all the loot in Lima ended up on Thompson's boats. Many of the Dons and Grandees who took their loot and attempted to escape to Spain were captured by pirates and their treasures taken.

A part of the Lima Treasure made it to Spain, but a ship carrying a large part of the treasure fell into the hands of a pirate named Benito de Soto (not to be confused with Benito Bonito). De Soto and his buccaneers buried this treasure on the island of Trinidad and then sailed north. They were captured by a Spanish man-o'-war and taken to Cuba.[5] Benito de Soto and most of his pirates were executed by the garotte. (Form of execution using a stick to twist a rope around the victims neck to cause slow strangulation.)

It was said that one pirate escaped to Calcutta and in 1848, near death, passed on the secret of the Trinidad treasure to his ship's captain who had nursed him during illness. This pirate died at Calcutta.[6] It is interesting to note that one of the syndicates in the early twentieth century put forward a letter claimed to be from Keating, which stated that Thompson had left for Calcutta after passing on his treasure map to Keating.

No doubt these promoters had gathered a collection of information which they fraudulently presented to investors as Keating's letter. Some of it accurate, and likely taken from a genuine Keating statement, and other parts were false, including the reference to Thompson leaving Newfoundland for Calcutta. Thompson had no involvement with Benito de Soto.[7]

5. Lloyd's records confirm pirates being captured and executed in Cuba. This is another part of the Trinidad Treasure story that has merged with the Thompson-Cocos Island story.
6. *The Romance of Treasure*, T.C. Bridges, 1931.
7. *Doubloons*, Charles H. Driscoll, 1931; and *The Lost Treasure (True Tales of Hidden Hoards)*, A. Hyatt Verril, 1930.

Chapter 9

Stevenson's Treasure Island Inspired by Lima Treasure Story

With so many similarities between the Lima Treasure story and Treasure Island, it is not surprising that authors, writers and television documentaries have focused on Cocos Island as the real 'Treasure Island', and the story of the Lost Treasure of Lima as Stevenson's inspiration for Treasure Island.

Treasure Island was originally called *The Sea Cook or Treasure Island*, and was first published in a magazine called *Young Folks*, as a series of feature columns in which Stevenson used the pseudonym Captain Richard North. James Henderson, *Young Folks* editor, dropped *Sea Cook* and went with the title *Treasure Island*. It was later revised and published in book form in Europe and the United States.

The Stevenson connection to the Keating story was something that intrigued me. Although to describe Silver, Stevenson drew from the physical features of his friend and agent, William Henley, a burly one-legged man, the character that emerged has multiple similarities to Captain John Keating.

Both Silver and Keating had found the treasure on two occasions and each took a small part of it home. Like Silver, Keating did not trust his wife and others. For example, it is believed that Keating murdered Captain William Boag, his friend and partner in the adventure.

Long John Silver was shrewd enough to outsmart his pirate friends and his wife, while Keating managed to outsmart his fellow Captains, a partner, two crews, relatives, friends and his wife.

In Stevenson's *Treasure Island*, Long John is associated with Captain Billy Bones, a name similar to Keating's friend, Captain Billy Boag. No doubt the name of one of Washington Irving's characters, Billy Bones came to mind when Stevenson was bringing Billy Boag into his tale of treasure and pirates.

Stevenson's story had young John Hawkins, while Keating had young Billy Boag, who was also in his late teens, and the son of Captain Billy Boag. Hawkins was haunted throughout his adult life by terrorizing memories of Long John Silver. Young Billy Boag had a lifetime of similar memories of Keating throwing Billy's father to the sharks.

In Keating's story, Captain Thompson in the *Mary Dear* steals the Treasure of Lima and buries it at Cocos Island. In *Treasure Island* there is Captain Flint of the *Walrus* who steals the treasure and buries it on Treasure Island.

In Stevenson's work there is mention of Corso Castle. In the Lima Treasure story there is the Callao Castle.

Courtesy Carter-Fitzgerald Black & White Photography

Jack Fitzgerald at the Queen Elizabeth II Library, Memorial University, comparing the story of the Lost Treasure of Lima, and Captain John Keating's adventure, with Robert Louis Stevenson's *Treasure Island*.

Stevenson mentions the pirate Captain Davis, who we know had buried gold on Cocos Island.

Stevenson describes the pirate ship, the *Walrus,* as "amuck with red blood and ready to sink with gold." The *Mary Dear* was covered in the blood of the murdered Royalist Guards and priests sent to guard the treasure. Like the *Walrus*, it carried an enormous treasure of gold, silver and gems that required ten longboats and four days to unload on shore.

The followers of Long John Silver turn on him and he seeks help from the doctor on the *Hispaniola*. When the *Edgecombe's* crew mutinies at Cocos Island, Keating and Boag enlist the support of Captain Gault in quieting the mutiny.

Stephenson's map has two small islands off the coast of the main island, while Cocos Island also has two small islands off its coast which are called the 'Dos Amigos Islands.' The map that Stevenson drew of Treasure Island for his son showed the island had only two, "...fine land-locked harbours, and a hill in the centre part marked, The Spy-glass Hill."[1] Cocos Island has only two accessible harbours: Chatham Bay and Wafer Bay. Also, there is on Cocos Island a hill called Observation Hill.

Treasure Island had a hermit living on the island named Ben Gun. Cocos Island had its true life Ben Gun in Augustus Gissler, who lived on the island for twenty years searching for the hidden treasure.

In the end, both Long John Silver and John Keating escaped justice.

While Stevenson's papers do not include any specific mention of the Lima Treasure, or of Captain John Keating and his partner, Captain Billy Bogue, it does contain what might be a clue to his real inspiration. Boag was not at all a common name, especially for a dog. Yet Stevenson had changed his pet Skye Terrier's name from Wattie to Bogue. B-o-g-u-e[2] was the spelling used in early writings on Keating and Boag, and it was the spelling that Charles Driscoll used in *Doubloons*. The dog was known to be ill-tempered and perhaps this trait reminded Stevenson of Keating's partner and victim, Billy Boag.

With so many similarities between the Lima Treasure story and *Treasure Island*, it is not surprising that writers, authors and television documentaries have focused on Cocos

1. *Treasure Island*, edited by Wendy R. Katz, p 43, 1994.
2. *The Teller of Tales, in search of Robert Louis Stevenson,* Davis Hunter, 1994.

Island as the real *Treasure Island*, and the true story of The
Lost Treasure of Lima as Stevenson's inspiration for *Treasure
Island*. Stevenson is believed to have become acquainted with
the Lima Treasure story while living in California.

Wendy R. Kratz, who edited the 1994 book *Treasure Island*
by Robert Louis Stevenson, wrote:

> It seems more likely that the island geography
> described in *Treasure Island* grew principally from
> Stevenson's experiences in California during 1879 and
> 1880 from where he returned to Scotland with his
> new wife and wrote his book, writing fifteen chapters
> in two weeks.

Stevenson also mentions the influence of California in his
inspiration to write *Treasure Island*. In his letter to Sidney
Colven[3] he writes, "The scenery for *Treasure Island* is
California in part, and in part chic."[4] There is little doubt that
once Stevenson began writing, he drew from his knowledge
of pirate adventure stories and writers like Washington Irving,
Daniel Defoe, Captain Charles Johnson and others for his
specific inspirations. However, it is widely believed that his
general inspiration was planted in his mind while living in
California.

San Francisco became a frequent launching port for expeditions to the island searching for the famous Lost Treasure of
Lima. Each venture returned empty handed but with many
stories of adventure to tell. San Francisco newspapers were
filled with stories of expeditions to Cocos Island. These expeditions began in the 1870s and continued for decades. While
Stevenson was in San Francisco the newspapers were filled
with stories of an expedition to Cocos Island that year. It is
unlikely that this true adventure story of maps, pirates, chests

---

3. Letters of Robert Louis Stevenson, Volume IV, p 300, cited in *Treasure Island*,
edited by Sir Sidney Colvin, 1905.
4. *Chic* refers to the popular belief of what an island used by pirates to hide buried
treasure might look like.

of gold, murder and intrigue had escaped the notice of Robert Louis Stevenson, who had a boyhood love of adventure.

California honored Stevenson's memory and his association with that state by naming a state park after him. The Robert Louis Stevenson State Park is located about a one-mile walk up Mount St. Helena and five miles from the summit. For his description of *Treasure Island*, Stevenson relied upon his memories of the Mount St. Helena area in California.

The Background to Writing of Treasure Island

Robert Louis Stevenson had no plans to write *Treasure Island* or any sort of pirate adventure. The trigger that changed his writing schedule was a spell of bad weather at Braemer, Scotland, during April, 1881. Stevenson, his wife and thirteen year old step-son Lloyd Osbourne were restricted to their cottage for several days of bad weather, and to relieve the boredom, Stevenson drew a map of an island he called Treasure Island.

The author then penned in piratical sounding names like Spy Glass Hill and Skeleton Island. He painted in the sea, and other main features using a shilling box of water colours.[5]

That evening Stevenson decided to write his tale of pirates and committed himself to writing a chapter a day. To do this he had set aside a feature he was writing about ghosts. After completing fifteen chapters in two weeks, he tired of the work and set the book aside until the following winter. That winter he took his family to Davos, Switzerland, where he hoped the weather would improve his health. While there he resumed writing his pirate story and completed the remaining nineteen chapters in fifteen days. He called the book *The Sea Cook or Treasure Island*.

During his writing of the book, he was visited by a friend named Dr. Alex Japp who, after reading the story, recom-

5. *Treasure Island*, Centennial Edition, edited by Wendy Kratz, 1994.

mended he send it to a popular boys magazine called *Young Folks*. Stevenson agreed, received thirty pounds for the work and was allowed to keep the copyright. The magazine's editor, a Mr. Henderson, dropped the Sea Cook part of the name and published the story in a series with the title *Treasure Island*. The final episode was published on June 28, 1882.

Encouraged by family and friends, Stevenson turned *Treasure Island* into a literary work. However, the book was turned down by two publishers. It was finally accepted in 1883 by Cassell Publishing, and in 1884 a United States edition went on the market. *Treasure Island* quickly became a world-wide classic.

While Stevenson's story of *Treasure Island* is a classic book that is known and loved world-wide, the story of Thompson, Keating, Fitzgerald and the other characters I've written about in this book is less well known and in many cases misrepresented. I believe that in this book I've been able to correct some misconceptions — and, I hope, place flesh upon the bare bones of some of the sailors, pirates, adventurers and legitimate businessmen whose connection to the treasures of Cocos Island has been lightly sketched in history. Like you, I'd like to be able to more accurately pinpoint the location of the treasures and to more fully separate fact from fiction and history from myth. I hope that the reader will see that I've been successful in my attempt to clarify some of the misconceptions and misunderstandings, but in the long run perhaps a mystery is more intriguing if it remains a mystery.

Author's Notes

Keating of the Cocos Island

Captain John Keating was born in Harbour Grace on February 18, 1808, the son of William Keating and Mary Connors. He had three brothers, William, James, and Patrick, and two sisters, Elizabeth and Alice. He moved to St. John's, where he worked as a ships' carpenter and sea captain. He married Elizabeth Power and they had one daughter, Margaret, born at St. John's on October 23, 1831. Margaret died in March, 1849, and Keating's wife passed away in June 1855. Both were buried at Belvedere Cemetery.

On July 5, 1871, he married Elizabeth Woods at St. John's. The sponsors at the wedding ceremony were George Trapnell and Anastasia Lacey. Captain Keating, or *Keating of the Cocos Island*, as he was called in St. John's, passed away on August 15, 1882. The only surviving Newfoundland record of his death is that which appeared in the *Newfoundland Gazette*. This record does not mention where he died and the Roman Catholic Church in St. John's, of which he was a member, did not keep burial records at the time. His deathbed statement was witnessed by two men who were Keating's neighbours in St. John's. This would indicate he died there. Burial records at Codroy — on the west coast of Newfoundland near Port aux Basques — were kept, but contain no record of his burial there. The Fitzgerald-Keating papers raise the possibility he might have died at Cape Breton, Nova Scotia.

The Keating name began appearing in records of Channel, Port aux Basques, NL, in 1871. After Keating's death, some Keatings in the Channel area moved to Westmount, Nova Scotia. Among those who made this move were John Keating, Mary Ellen Keating, Nora Keating and Cecilia Keating. Mary Ellen married Arthur Johnson Petch, and Nora married Gerard Gothier. Their marriage records from Westmount have been attached to parish records at Channel. Captain John Keating may have had business interests in Cape Breton.

Channel, Port aux Basques

Channel was an area of Port aux Basques where Keating had business interests. It was the most westerly settlement of importance in the Newfoundland electoral district of Burgeo-LaPoile. Considerable trade was carried out there with several mercantile establishments. Inhabitants fished for cod and halibut. It was the centre where mail was dropped off and picked up and also a port of entry and last station of the western steam route. It is fifteen miles by boat from Rose Blanche, where there was a large Keating merchant business, and three hundred miles from St. John's by steamer. The population of Channel in 1882 was 600. Codroy, where Fitzgerald met Keating in 1882, had a population of 415, but there were no Keatings among its population.

The Boags

There were very few Boags in Newfoundland in the nineteenth century. They are believed to have emigrated here from Scotland. The first record of a Boag in St. John's was that of Myles Boag, who came to Newfoundland in 1809 and had a daughter born there in that year. James Boag, possibly a brother of Captain William Boag, Keating's partner in the treasure hunting adventure, was a partner in the shipping firm of Perchard and Boag. (Richard Perchard and James Boag).

When the firms of James/Thomas Boag and Richard Perchard became Perchard and Boag, they had a total of fifty-four ships, one of which was the *Water Witch*, a famous Newfoundland vessel. Boag brought sixteen ships into the partnership and Perchard brought thirty-eight ships.

The firm owned the *George Henry Harrison,* which Captain William Boag Sr. commanded in 1840.

Captain William Boag Jr. later became Captain of the *J & C Jost* (1856).

Captain William Boag Sr.'s daughter married Charles Hutchings, who became a lawyer, Inspector General of the Newfoundland Constabulary and a court judge.

Captain Nick Fitzgerald

In an effort to more clearly identify Captain Nick Fitzgerald, I present the following information from genealogical records at the Provincial Archives of Newfoundland and Labrador. Captain Nicholas was the son of Morris Fitzgerald and Johanna Connors. They married on January 25, 1835, and Nicholas was born in 1839 at Harbour Grace. His sponsors were Morris Lahey and Ellen Moriarity. His grandparents were James Fitzgerald and Anne Cash.

Captain Nick's father, Morris, was born in March, 1811. He had a sister, Isabella, born on April 22, 1809 and a brother, Michael, born on December 19, 1808. Captain William Fitzgerald of Carbonear may have been a relative of Captain Nicholas Fitzgerald.

One year prior to being shipwrecked and meeting Captain John Keating, Captain Nick Fitzgerald was at the Labrador fishery in command of the *George T. Fogg.*

Captain Nicholas Fitzgerald had six children. Two died from whooping cough in 1870, within months of each other. Fitzgerald was survived by his wife, three daughters, and one son. At the time of Fitzgerald's death in 1907, there was a Patrick Fitzgerald operating a business on Water Street in Harbour Grace. According to the Newfoundland Directory for that year, Patrick was the son of Nicholas Fitzgerald.

Lord Thomas Cochrane and a Stolen Treasure

Lord Thomas Cochrane was born on December 14, 1775, and died on October 11, 1860. He was a politician and naval adventurer. Cochrane was one of the most daring and successful captains of the Napoleonic Wars and the French nicknamed him "le loup des mers" (the sea wolf). His life and exploits served as inspiration for the naval fiction of the twentieth century novelists C. S. Forester and Patrick O'Brian. The fictional career of Horatio Hornblower was based on that of Lord Cochrane. Another novelist, Bernard Cornwall, featured Cochrane as himself in his book *Sharpe's Devil.*

Just as there were two Thompson's who caused confusion in the 'Lima Treasure' story, there were two Lord Thomas Cochranes. Both served in the Royal Navy with distinction, both having joined at an early age. Both served terms in the British Parliament. Both were active in the Royal Navy at the time the Lima Treasure was pirated.

The Lord Thomas Cochrane who became a central figure in the Lima Treasure story was the "10th Earl of Dundonald". The other Lord Cochrane served as Governor of Newfoundland from 1825 to 1834. The Earl was the son of Sir Archibald Cochrane, while the other Lord Cochrane was son of Admiral Sir Alexander Cochrane. The Newfoundland Governor Thomas Cochrane was likely the nephew of the Earl of Dundonald.

Over the past hundred years, the former Newfoundland Governor was sometimes mistaken for the 10th Earl of Dundonald. The Earl served as commander of the Chilean Navy from 1817-1822. In 1832 he became Vice Admiral and Commander-in-Chief of the North American station. He became Admiral in the Royal Navy in 1851. The other Lord Cochrane became an Admiral in 1865.

Lord Cochrane's experience with the British Navy would have acquainted him with knowledge of Benito Bonito's pirate activities. In December 1820, Cochrane captured the

Spanish man-of-war, the *Esmeralda,* at Callao, an act which weakened Royalist Forces protecting Lima.

In 1846, Lord Thomas Cochrane was still fighting pirates. In that year, at the request of the Sultan of Borneo, the British government sent twenty-six ships, with 500 men under Cochrane's command, to seek out an Arabian pirate named Sharif Ousman and his seven ships. Ousman had been terrorizing shipping off the coast of Borneo. (*The Newfoundlander,* March 9, 1846)

Benito Bonito

Benito Bonito was an officer on a Brazilian privateer under the command of a Portuguese captain. In 1818, he led a mutiny off Cuba during which the Captain was murdered. In the following few days he captured a slave ship and murdered all on board except two of the youngest crew members. Lloyd's records describe a situation similar to the Bonito story in the same year the Bonito event happened, and which names the privateer ship as the *Pelican.* The *Pelican* taken by the pirates was 124 tons.

Bonito had a practice of recruiting new pirates to man ships taken by him, which he intended for use in his illegal operations.

The *Edgecombe*

Some authors claimed that the *Edgecombe,* along with all people on board, was lost during a storm encountered when going round the Horn in 1841. This is inaccurate. The following shipping movements of the *Edgecombe* are taken from the Lloyd's Shipping Records from 1841 to 1844:

> January 25, 1841 — left St. John's for Rio de Janeiro, the Falklands, and arrived in June at Cocos Island.

March 3, 1841 — arrived at Rio de Janeiro.
April 9, 1841 — left Rio de Janeiro and
went around the Horn for Port Louis, Berkley
Sound, east Falkland Islands.
June 14, 1841 — left east Falkland Islands,
and according to Boag family records, arrived
at Cocos Island on June 18, 1841.
October 22, 1842 — arrived at Liverpool,
England, from Panama. The ship did not
return to St. John's, Newfoundland, as other
authors claimed.
1843 — went to Havana, Cuba under
Captains Gibson and Tomkins.
1844 — took cargo to and from Africa.

It is not known whether the *Edgecombe* returned to Cocos
Island to search for treasure. It is very probable that Captain
Gault did take the *Edgecombe* back to search for the treasure,
but Keating had taken the treasure map, and it is not likely the
treasure was found.

Job Brothers, merchants of St. John's who engaged the
Edgecombe to take a half cargo of fish to Rio de Janeiro, were
amused to find out that the real purpose of the vessel's trip to
South America was to search for the Lost Treasure of Lima.
Soon after learning of the story, they christened one of their
ships *The Lima.*

The *Devonshire* becomes the *Mary Dear*

I believe that the *Devonshire*, which was captured by Bonito,
had its name changed to the *Mary Dear*. When Bonito moved
to the Pacific area, he did so using the *Relampago* and the
Devonshire. When he abandoned seventeen men at Valparaiso,
Chili, he left the *Devonshire* behind under command of
Captain Marion Thompson. There has been conflicting information regarding the *Devonshire*, likely because there were five

other vessels with the same name in the period between 1814 and 1821. The following information is taken from Lloyd's of London, Records:

> Devonshire — 76 tons — French owned — Captain J. Agland.
> Devonshire — 130 tons — British owned — Captain R. Day.
> Devonshire — 60 tons — Scottish Registry — Captain P. Gibbons.
> Devonshire — 94 tons — British owned — Captain Johnston.
> Devonshire — 305 tons — Spanish owned — operating out of Brazil — Captain J. Guthrie.

The *Devonshire (Mary Dear)* used by Bonito in 1820, and again by Thompson in 1821, was the *Devonshire* taken from Captain J. Guthrie, and weighed 305 tons. By 1821, only two of the five *Devonshires* remained. Two were lost at sea and the third taken by Bonito. It would have taken a large ship to carry the loot from Lima, ten longboats, along with a twelve-man crew, guards, and priests from the Lima Cathedral. The *Devonshire,* at 305 tons, was ideal for the job.

Montmorency Suggestion

In his 1904 book, *On the Track of Treasure*, Montmorency suggested that it was Captain William Boag — not Captain Keating — who found the hiding place of the Lima Treasure. He claimed he was told by a Swedish sailor, who had also searched for the treasure, that he had found a tree with the letter 'K' etched into it and an arrow pointing to the bottom of the tree. The Swede searched the area and recovered a Spanish gold coin from the time of King Charles III of Spain, dated 1788. Based on this the Swede concluded that Boag had found the treasure and had removed some of it. Keating surprised him when he was trying to hide it, and when Boag refused to tell him where the treasure cave with the Lima loot was located, he killed Boag. According to Montmorency, this would explain why Keating never recovered the entire treasure. The author suggested that the purpose of Keating's second trip had been to recover the portion of the treasure Boag had hidden by that tree.

However, this claim has no validity. Boag family records show that Boag and Keating left Cocos Island together and went to Panama, where Boag died under mysterious circumstances. From Panama Keating returned to Newfoundland. Boag's son Billy was on the *Edgecombe* expedition and returned to his home in Newfoundland to tell the true story.

Lost Treasures

Those interested in hidden and unclaimed treasures will find the following list of lost treasures interesting. At today's values, the combined total of this sampling of lost treasure would be in the billions of dollars.

Name	Date	Location	Value
Unidentified	1572	Off Campos, Brazil	$121,000,000
Unidentified	1702	Vigo Bay, Spain	$140,000,000
Unidentified	1716	Table Bay, South Africa	$100,000,000
Unidentified	1827	Navarino Bay, Greece	$70,000,000
Unidentified	1628	Matansas Bay, Cuba	$30,000,000

Name	Date	Location	Value
Golden Hind	1578	Island of Plate, off Ecuador	$20,000,000
San Fernando	1597	Pt. Du Cap, St. Lucia Is. (B.W.I.)	$20,000,000
Good Jesus	1598	Porto Bello, Harbourm Panama	$2,000,000
Santa Cecilia	1702	Juan Fernados Island, off Chile	$5,000,000
Unidentified	1715	Near Long Key, Florida	$65,000,000
Santissim Conception	1775	Tortuga Bay, Haiti	$5,000,000
De Braak	1798	Old Kiln Roads, Del.	$15,000,000
San Pedro de Alcantara	1815	South of Margharita Island, Venezuela	$5,000,000
Unidentified	1820	Off Bradford, Florida	$5,000,000
Admiral De Grasse	1782	Off Cape Engano, Dom. Republic	$5,000,000
Merida	1911	Virginia Capes, Va.	$5,500,000
Grosvenor	1781	Salt River, South Africa	$5,500,000

Name	Date	Location	Value
Telemarque	1790	Seine River, France	$20,000,000
Black Prince	1854	Balaclava Bay, Black Sea	$5,000,000
George Sand	1863	Off Pratus Shoals, China	$13,000,000
Phantom	1862	Off Hong Kong, China	$10,000,000
Hampshire	1916	Off Marwick Head, North Sea	$9,500,000

Bibliography

Registers, Documents and Newspapers

Maritime History Archives: Memorial University, St. John's, NL

Newfoundland Directories. Hunter Library, St. John's, NL

Newfoundland Census Records

The Newfoundlander: 1837 to 1860

City of St. John's Archives

Church Records-Baptismal, Marriages, and Deaths;
Provincial Archives of Newfoundland and Labrador

.

Places Visited

Mount Carmel Cemetery, St. John's, NL

Belvedere Cemetery, St. John's, NL

General Protestant Cemetery, St. John's, NL

Anglican Cemetery, St. John's, NL

Bay Bulls Cemetery, Bay Bulls, NL

Cemetery at the Gun Ridge, Bay Bulls, NL

Roman Catholic Cemetery, Harbour Grace, NL

Roman Catholic Cemetery, North Sydney, NS

Harbour Grace Museum, NL

Newfoundland Museum, NL

Captain Bob Bartlett Heritage Home and Museum, Brigus, NL

Cupid's Museum, NL

Interviews

Dr. Ina Knobloch, Frankfurt, Germany - at St. John's, NL, July 2004

Richard Hartery, Mount Pearl, NL, November 2004

Catherine Cahill, St. John's, NL, November 2004

Books and Publications

Bridges, T. C. 1931. *The Romance of Buried Treasure*. London: Nisbet.

Coffman. F.L. 1957. *1001 Lost, Buried or Sunken Treasures*. New York: Thomas Nelson & Sons.

Colvin, Sir Sidney. Ed. 1905. *The Letters of Robert Louis Stevenson. Vol. II.* MI: Thomson Gale.

Crocker, William J. 1998. *Tracking Treasure: In Search of East Coast Burnaby*. Halifax: Nimbus.

Crowell, Thomas Y. 1930. *The Pacific*. New York: Company Publishers.

Davies, Hunter. 1994. *The Teller of Tales: In Search of Robert Louis Stevenson.* Massachusetts: Interlink.

Devine, Patrick Kevin. 1936. "The Cocos Island Treasure" *Newfoundland Quarterly*.

Driscoll, C. .B. 1931. *Doubloons: The Story of Buried Treasure*. London: Chapman & Hall.

Fitzgerald, Jack. 2002. *Beyond Belief: Incredible Stories of Old St. John's.* St. John's: Creative Book Publishing.

Furneaux, Rupert. 1968. *The Great Treasure Hunts.* London: Hamlyn Publishing.

Hutchings, C. .H. 1908. "The Cocos Island Treasure" *Newfoundland Quarterly* 8 (3): 9-10.

Katz, Wendy R. 1994. *Treasure Island.* Ed. Wendy R. Katz. Edinburgh: Edinburgh UP.

Kinsbruner, Jay. 1994. *Independence In Spanish America-Civil Wars, Revolutions and Underdevelopment.* Albuquerque: U of New Mexico P. 75-95.

Lynch, John. 1994. *Latin American Revolutions 1808-1826: Old and New World Origins.* London: U of Oklahoma P.

Nesmith, Robert I. 1958. *Dig for Pirate Treasure.* New York: Devin-Adair

Nowlan, Michael O., & Dr. Harry D. Roberts. 1982. *The Newfoundland Fish Boxes: A Chronicle of the Fishery.* New Brunswick: Brunswick Press.

O'Hanlon, Betty. 1964. "The Lost Loot of Lima" *The Atlantic Advocate* 54 (10): 32-35.

Paine, Ralph D. 1922. *The Book of Buried Treasure.* New York: McMillan.

Prago, Albert. 1970. *The Revolution In Spanish America 1808-1825.* New York: McMillan.

Rodriguez, James E. 1998. *The Independence of Spanish America.* New York: Cambridge UP.

Smallwood, Joseph R. *Encyclopedia of Newfoundland.*

Snow, Edward Rowe. 1953. *The Tales of Pirates and Their Gold.* New York: Dodd-Mead.

Verril, A. Hyatt. 1930. *Lost Treasure: True Tales of Hidden Hoards.* New York: D. Appleton.

Wilson, Derek. 1981. *The World Atlas of Treasure*. London: Pan Books. William Collin's Sons.

Worcester, Donald E. 1915. *Bolivar*. Toronto: Little Brown.